ছ ছ ছ ছ ছ

Songs of Love, Poems of Sadness

Songs of Love, Poems of Sadness

THE EROTIC VERSE OF THE SIXTH DALAI LAMA

Translated from the Tibetan, with an introductory
essay and notes for appreciation by

Paul Williams

I.B. TAURIS
LONDON · NEW YORK

Published in 2004 by I.B.Tauris & Co. Ltd
6 Salem Road, London W2 4BU
175 Fifth Avenue, New York, NY 10010
www.ibtauris.com

In the United States of America and Canada distributed by Palgrave Macmillan,
a division of St Martin's Press, 175 Fifth Avenue, New York, NY 10010

ISBN: 1 85043 479 4
EAN: 978 1 85043 479 5

A full CIP record for this book is available from the British Library
A full CIP record for this book is available from the Library of Congress

Library of Congress catalog card: available

Typeset in Junius Modern by A. & D. Worthington, Newmarket, Suffolk
Printed and bound in Great Britain by TJ International Ltd, Padstow, Cornwall

ཨ ཨ ཨ ཨ ཨ

Contents

For Sharon, Myrddin, Tiernan and Tārā

– my lovely family, forever.

ཆ ཆ ཆ ཆ ཆ

Acknowledgements

This translation could not have been undertaken without the first critical edition of the Tibetan text, prepared by Per Sorensen. The text reproduced here is taken from his book, *Divinity Secularized: An Inquiry into the Nature and Form of the Songs Ascribed to the Sixth Dalai Lama* (Vienna, 1990). I am in total debt to Sorensen's devoted work, which includes extensive notes based on a formidable understanding of this sort of Indo-Tibetan literature. Anyone intending a proper study of the Sixth Dalai Lama's verses needs must have constant recourse to this comprehensive contribution, if only to disagree with it.

It is all the more astonishing, therefore, to find that other translations of the Sixth Dalai Lama's verses, even those undertaken since 1990, show no sign at all of ever having heard of Sorensen's work.

ཀྲ ཀྲ ཀྲ ཀྲ ཀྲ

Introduction

Everyone who studies closely the Sixth Dalai Lama (1683–1706) becomes obsessed by him. His ghost – or a 'manifested body' – is said to have frequented the audiences of the Seventh and the Thirteenth Dalai Lamas.[1] In his poetry he advances towards us – but then he shrinks, as if to say 'Leave me to myself. Go away. I have had enough of your demands on me. I didn't ask for it. What right do you have to make me your Dalai Lama? What right have you to endeavour to make me a eunuch, while still leaving my body and my passions intact?' Other Dalai Lamas have been great scholars, powerful politicians or simply Buddhist monks that died young before they could make much impact. Perhaps the current Fourteenth Dalai Lama is a saint. But only the Sixth refused to take full monastic vows, returned the vows he had taken already, and loved women, alcohol and archery (maybe like modern computer or role-playing games) with a passion that shows perhaps a vague premonition of his early death at the age of 24. That is, if he really did die then. One tradition has it that he survived in relative obscurity for a further 40 years. He also wrote love poetry, poetry that has survived in a Tibetan world where secular verse generally does not, precisely because he was the Dalai Lama.

But surely (some say) it must all have a deeper meaning than simply love of lovely young women? He was, after all, the Dalai Lama. Surely it must all be tantric sexual yoga or radical political protest. Or both. But in this poetry we see the real heart of a young man thrust into the central political position of a theocracy that was not of his making and that he scarcely understood. That is, of course, if the poetry is really by him.

You see – he advances towards us and then he retreats. His is the saddest story in Tibetan history prior to the modern era – when (alas) the whole of Tibet has become one involuntary tragedy.

Who or what is a Dalai Lama?

Tsangyang Gyatso, the Sixth Dalai Lama, was intended to be head of the Tibetan state and a celibate Buddhist monk. He disappeared in 1706 while under Mongol military escort. It was given out that he had died of illness, but he was thought by some to have been murdered. As we have seen, one story has the Sixth Dalai Lama living incognito and devoutly for a further 40 years. At the time of his disappearance he was still in his early 20s.

Tsangyang Gyatso left behind him a racy reputation with the young women of Lhasa, the capital city of Tibet, and a small collection of unique love poetry.

In this Introduction I want to try to help readers new to the love poems of the Sixth Dalai Lama to appreciate how extraordinary they are. And I would like to do this first by trying to give you an idea of how a Dalai Lama is seen from the *inside*, within the tradition of Tibetan Buddhism. But for readers who are reasonably familiar with Buddhism, or those who just want to know my conclusions, I suggest you turn to the summary at the end of this section and read on from there.

It is common of course for the Dalai Lama of Tibet to be referred to in popular parlance as a 'god-king'. This is, however, very misleading. Buddhism believes in any number of 'gods' (*deva*-s). To be a 'god' (or a 'goddess') is not Buddhist enlightenment. It is a type of rebirth. In infinite cycles of rebirths we have all been gods many times. Gods are beings who in general have a pleasant enough life if one admires the hedonistic indulgences of Hollywood film stars. A 'god' lives the spiritually vacuous life of a playboy or playgirl in some other rather pleasant world called a 'heaven'. But Buddhism denies altogether the existence of a loving creator God, a Necessary Being, as understood in the great theistic world religions such as Christianity or Islam. Such a God could not possibly actually exist.[2]

To be a 'king', on the other hand, is in Buddhism a secular lay occupation seen very much as part of the realm of unenlightenment (*saṃsāra*), spiritual immaturity. If we do conclude that nevertheless a Dalai Lama is in some sense a king, it should at least be on his own terms, which are the terms of Tibetan Buddhism.

So how is a Dalai Lama seen from the inside, from within the tradition of Tibetan Buddhism? I shall begin by trying to convey how the present Dalai Lama, the Fourteenth, is seen by other Tibetans and how he sees himself. This is to start where a contemporary Tibetan teacher – indeed the Dalai Lama himself – would want to start.

One's religion, as it relates to the individual, is for the Tibetan Buddhist tradition a matter of *motivation*. Its purpose in the final analysis in one way or another is seen as the achievement of complete, supreme happiness. Thus in the Tibetan vision Buddhism is thought to be a very direct practical matter of working on the present state of who we are, pre-eminently our minds. This is in order to bring about a transformation away from what Buddhism calls the 'three root poisons' of greed, hatred and delusion towards their opposites, altruism, loving kindness and wisdom. Which strategies are most suitable to bring about this transformation depend on the present situation of the individuals concerned just as, Buddhists say, which medicine is suitable to bring about physical health depends upon the illness and its present modality.

It was the Indian missionary Atiśa who, in the eleventh century, when asked by his Tibetan hosts for a direct and down-to-earth practical teaching, provided the framework into which so many later generations of Tibetan scholars and holy men have sought to fit the spiritual path. It is this framework that lies in the background of the present Dalai Lama's own vision of himself, his role and message. It is a framework familiar to most Tibetans, since lamas – teachers, gurus – repeat it at the commencement of just about all their teachings. This framework is that of the 'three types of person' (Tibetan: *skyes bu gsum*). It is based on what a Buddhist sees as the three types of ruling motivation. These are motivations that a person might have not only in the spiritual life but also in all life's activities.

The person of lowest motivation, Atiśa says, is one whose concern in life is with personal gain. This is 'one who strives for his or her own benefit, concerned only with the pleasures of the realm of unenlightenment (*saṃsāra*)'. In other words, if we were honest, this might be thought to be most of us. The concern here is with personal worldly pleasure, whether of a crass sort or the more refined pleasures of fame, pride in a job well done or aesthetic relish. Seeking to attain heaven would also be seen by our Buddhists as belonging to this category. A higher motivation is that usually associated by Westerners, if inaccurately, with Buddhist monks and nuns, 'those who have turned their backs on the pleasures of unenlightenment, turned away definitively from wrong actions, and strive taking as a goal simply their own peace'. That is, they aim for *nirvāṇa*, liberation or enlightenment, the end for themselves of all suffering and rebirth. This is the middle motivation. It integrates a deep sense of right and wrong, which might be found even among those of the lowest motivation, with an even deeper and radical renunciation of the world and indeed all worlds of rebirth (including that of the 'gods' and their heavens) in favour of enlightenment. But noble and rare though this motivation is, Tibetans will all say there is something higher. It is something that like the previous motivations is open to all sentient beings and not just human beings. It is something that many aspire to but few really achieve in this life. Atiśa continues: 'Someone who wishes by all means truly to bring an end to all the sufferings of others ... that person is Supreme.'[3]

In its fullest expression Tibetan Buddhism holds that all the actions of the supreme person are motivated by pure altruism. Such a person, who makes no ultimate distinction between his or her own sufferings, his or her own happiness, and those of others, but who strives no matter what it may cost to eliminate the suffering of everyone is called a *bodhisattva*. The goal of the bodhisattva is no ordinary enlightenment, no nirvana as it is understood by those of the middling motivation. Rather it is said to be full, perfect Buddhahood. This is the state of those who have attained what is for Buddhism the fullest expansion consciousness is capable of, expressed as the complete perfection of wisdom and (and this is crucial) compassion.

This is known as *Mahāyāna Buddhism*, and it is the form of Buddhism that Tibetans ultimately aspire to. Thus Mahāyāna Buddhism – the Great (*mahā*) Way (or Vehicle: *yāna*) of the bodhisattva – is held properly not to be a matter of doctrines, rituals or vestments, but fundamentally a matter of motivation. Truly to have this motivation, to have what is called the compassionate 'awakening mind' or 'mind of enlightenment' (*bodhicitta*) possessed by the bodhisattva is for Mahāyāna Buddhism perhaps akin to the conversion experience in certain forms of Christianity, albeit much rarer. It is held to be a complete transformation, a complete revolution away from egoistic preoccupation to altruism. The Indian Śāntideva, the great poet of altruism, wrote in the eighth century of this awakening mind in his *Bodhicaryāvatāra* ('A Guide to the Buddhist Path to Awakening'), probably the work that has had the most influence on the present Dalai Lama:

> That jewel, the Mind, which is the seed of pure happiness in the world and the remedy for the suffering of the world, how at all can its merit be measured?[4]

Thus the concern of a real bodhisattva is thought finally to be solely with the benefit of others. He or she wishes for Buddhahood only because Buddhahood offers the completion of that transformation into a being not only perfectly altruistic but also with perfect power, perfect *ability*, to help others. That being is called a *Buddha*. It is the fulfilment of intention and act. For the bodhisattva there is held to be no personal (in some way still selfish) gain in the attainment of Buddhahood. Any personal gain no matter how refined reaches its fulfilment in the second motivation. Indeed the bodhisattva does not even shun rebirth. The bodhisattva welcomes rebirth if it can be used to benefit others. Perhaps the current Dalai Lama's favourite verse in all the thousands of Buddhist scriptures, the one he quotes most often and holds most perfectly to articulate his own spiritual aspirations, is also from Śāntideva:

> As long as space abides and as long as the world abides, so long may I abide, destroying the sufferings of the world.[5]

This, the Dalai Lama would hold, expresses one dimension – he would say the most important dimension – of what he really is. He is a bodhisattva.

This bodhicitta, the so-called 'awakening mind' of a bodhisattva, is not something that just happens. The Tibetan traditions prescribe a set series of meditations, each to be adopted at the appropriate stage in the spiritual path, which will eventually issue in this inner revolution.[6] These meditations, and this revolution, the Fourteenth Dalai Lama says he knows he has undergone in many previous lives. Although, he points out, generally spiritual practitioners do not speak publicly about their inner experiences, still he states after quoting the verse from Śāntideva above: 'I have that wish in this lifetime, and I know that I had that wish in past lifetimes.'[7] This wish, he states elsewhere, 'we should have … from the depths of our heart, as if nailed there'. And it 'is not merely concerned with a few sentient beings such as friends and relatives, but extends up to the limits of the cosmos, in all directions and towards all beings throughout space.'[8]

It is normal among Tibetan Buddhists to consider that the Dalai Lama has truly actualized this awakening mind. He is thought really to be a developed bodhisattva. Thus the Dalai Lama strives to act for the benefit of others in the light of vows he has taken as a devout Mahāyāna practitioner. It may not be easy. The current Dalai Lama's younger brother, Tendzin Chögyal, who, like the Dalai Lama, is held to be the reincarnation of a great teacher, left the monastic order and married. At one time he was in the Indian Army. From the point of view of Buddhist doctrine none of this need necessarily be incompatible with being the reincarnation of a great Buddhist teacher, a bodhisattva acting for the benefit of others in ways that may not be obvious to those of us with lesser insight. Nevertheless Tendzin Chögyal has been very critical of the institution of incarnate lamas (sprul sku, pronounced 'trulku') which has for centuries been an integral part of Tibetan Buddhism. While aspiring to help others – the bodhisattva ideal is so strong in Tibet that all or most Tibetans say they aspire to help others – Tendzin Chögyal has observed in an interview that personally he is not a Mahāyānist. This will appear a paradoxical statement to those who think that all Tibetan Buddhism is Mahāyānist. But from the Tibetan perspective, while most Tibetans aspire to be true Mahāyāna bodhisattvas, Tendzin Chögyal was perhaps just being honest. He did not feel that he had genuinely developed that awakening mind. He is therefore not of the Supreme Motivation, even if he *is* an 'incarnate lama'.[9] Perhaps it was Tendzin Chögyal who made the comment attributed simply to 'one of the Dalai Lama's close relations' that 'for Him [the Dalai Lama] everything is easy. He has resolved all the paradoxes, because He is a bodhisattva. For the rest of us, it is a different story!'[10]

So the Dalai Lama considers himself, and is considered by other Tibetans, to be a bodhisattva. And the bodhisattva is held to be willing to be reborn any number of times in order to fulfil his vow of helping others. Eventually he will attain perfect Buddhahood and then be able perfectly to help others. But the Dalai Lama is also what Tibetans call a 'trulku', and to be a trulku, an incarnate or reincarnate lama, is more than just this. It is to occupy a very particular place and role in the Tibetan religious vision. It is a vision that also embraces the Tibetan picture of society and even politics.

It is often said that a trulku, an incarnate lama, is a lama who has been discovered, usually as a young child, to be the reincarnation of a specific named lama who had previously died. The trulku is taken back to his (or 'her' – but with few exceptions always 'his') monastery or home base and trained to re-adopt his old religious position. Broadly speaking this picture is correct. But in Buddhism very little is ever simple. What we are interested in here is the Tibetans' own picture of what a trulku is, and what is involved in being a trulku, with particular reference to the central figure of the whole system, the Dalai Lama.

First, something about the Tibetan words involved. There is little problem regarding the etymology and origin of the Tibetan expression *sprul sku* (trulku). It is made up of two words: *sprul*, which is connected with transforming or transformation, or actively changing, even 'bringing about in an apparently miraculous way', and *sku*, which is the Tibetan honorific form of the word for body.[11] Thus etymologically and literally the *sprul sku* is a 'transformation body' which, with the honorific, indicates its connection with honoured beings, Buddhas and sometimes very spiritually advanced bodhisattvas. It corresponds to the Sanskrit word *nirmāṇakāya*, which is a well-known expression of Indian Mahāyāna Buddhology referring to the various emanated forms sent out by what may be called the Buddha's 'glorified form'. This second type of body is a glorified form (*saṃbhogakāya*, or *sāṃbhogikakāya* – 'Enjoyment Body') that unlike the transformation bodies appears not in this world among beings like us, but in a Pure Land. The Pure Land is a transcendent abode – a 'Buddha Land' – where a Mahāyāna Buddha (for it is held that there are very many of them) sits in glory teaching the Mahāyāna. Such a Land can be visited by bodhisattvas of sufficient meditative power to reach through their spiritual development to such an exalted space. The myriad emanated forms occur out of the compassion of the Buddhas. They exist in order to bring about the benefit of those who are to be helped spiritually and materially and who are not sufficiently advanced to benefit directly from the glorified body of a Buddha, a Buddha's supreme and extra-terrestrial physical form. There are various classifications of transformation bodies, but essentially they are emanations of a Buddha occurring without partiality or exception in whatever form is appropriate in order to help sentient beings.[12] Advanced bodhisattvas, to a lesser degree, are also held to have this ability of emanation. One Mahāyāna scripture typically speaks of very many bodhisattvas, including the renowned Avalokiteśvara. He is one of a number of named bodhisattvas who are considered so advanced, so possessed of miraculous abilities that can be cultivated by one on the spiritual path in order to help others, that they have become in effect supramundane helpers. Avalokiteśvara is held to be the veritable essence of compassion, working tirelessly for the benefit of others. In the scripture he declares that:

> I appear in the midst of the activities of all sentient beings without leaving the presence of all buddhas, and take care of them. ...
> I also develop sentient beings by appearing in various forms ... by magically producing various forms ... by appearing to them as members of their own various races and conditions, and by living together with them.[13]

It is Avalokiteśvara, often held by Tibetans to be already a Buddha rather than an advanced bodhisattva, who is said to have a very close and special connection with the Dalai Lamas. What the nature of that connection is remains to be seen. But first, back to the trulkus.

We have seen that the primary and original meaning of *sprul sku* is an emanation from a Buddha for the practical purposes of compassion. The late Song Rinpoche, himself a distinguished *sprul sku* lama of the Dalai Lama's dGe lugs (pronounced 'Geluk') school, has commented that properly speaking this is the correct use of the word *trulku*. But clearly all the many thousands of trulkus, 'incarnate lamas', of Tibetan Buddhism cannot all be emanations from supramundane, transcendent Buddhas or bodhisattvas. Those who go by the name of *sprul sku*-s in contemporary Tibetan Buddhism, Song Rinpoche observed, should really be called *yang srid* (pronounced 'yangsi'), which is to say simply 'again becomings' (Sanskrit: *punarbhava*). That is, they are literally 'reincarnations', 'born agains'.[14] But they are by no means necessarily thought to be emanations of a Buddha or an advanced bodhisattva.

In fact, in practice, in everyday contemporary Tibetan, the term *sprul sku* (trulku) is ambiguous. It has come to have two uses. It is listed as such in the encyclopaedic 'Great Tibetan–Chinese Dictionary', the *Bod rgya tshig mdzod chen mo*. Along with the sense of (i) an emanation of a Buddha or a bodhisattva, this second meaning of *sprul sku*, a separate though related meaning, is given as a derived expression for simply the *yang srid*. It is (ii) simply any reincarnation of a high-ranking lama.[15] In order to preserve some distinction the specific sense of a Buddha or bodhisattva emanation is sometimes captured by another expression, the term *sprul pa* (pronounced 'trulba').[16] So we find that the great rJe Tsong kha pa, the late fourteenth-century founder of the Dalai Lama's dGe lugs school, is held to have attained such an elevated state that although he has no reincarnation lineage (i.e. any *yang srid*-s), he still has emanations. He is thought to be still emanating as a Buddha in order to help others. His failure to reincarnate is not thought of as indicating a deficiency in compassion. It is rather merely an alternative response to the sufferings of sentient beings.

There is no doubt that in his mind and the minds of most Tibetans the Dalai Lama is a *yang srid*, a reincarnation. In a sense, for Buddhism we are all reincarnations. But a *yang srid* like the Dalai

Lama is different, for he is also a *trulku* in the more general and colloquial sense of the term (the second sense given above). The present Dalai Lama has explained that there are four types of birth:

> (A) The first is the ordinary rebirth of those with no relevant spiritual mastery. Such beings – most of us, I suppose – have no power to determine their rebirths. They are influenced solely by the force of previous deeds, previous *karman*.
>
> (B) There is, however, another type of rebirth, that 'of one who due to past spiritual attainment, can choose, or at least influence, the place and situation of rebirth'.[17]

I want to dwell for a moment on the distinction between these two types of birth. I shall return to the third and fourth types later. In the second case reincarnation can become in its clearest exemplification a matter of conscious decision and control. In the case of a bodhisattva, of course, this is a conscious decision to return in order to benefit others in accordance with his or her bodhisattva aspiration. There are meditation practices that are held to make this possible, actually to be able to control one's process of rebirth. Moreover from perhaps the end of the thirteenth century in Tibet the idea evolved that if a bodhisattva had sufficient spiritual mastery to control his or her rebirth, it ought also to be possible to identify that child who is the reincarnation.[18] Thus is becomes possible to train the child to re-adopt his or her old place in the religious system; hence the phenomenon of trulkus in the more general and colloquial sense of the term (sense (ii) above). These are 'incarnate lamas', of which, the Dalai Lama has said, there were probably a few thousand in old Tibet before the Chinese occupation, and even now there are still a few hundred.[19]

Those who can determine their rebirths are certainly trulkus in this colloquial sense. But in spite of what is often thought by Westerners and Tibetans alike, not all trulkus are held to be able to determine their rebirths. A contemporary Tibetan lama, Doboom Tulku (i.e. 'trulku'), has commented that there are different types of trulkus. First there are trulkus of Buddhas and bodhisattvas. He presumably refers here to 'trulkus' in the proper, primary sense (sense (i) above) – emanations, or transformation bodies, of the Buddhas and very advanced bodhisattvas. Second, Doboom Tulku comments, are those 'who have accumulated good karma, due to which they are very helpful to other sentient beings in preaching … and so on'. And finally we come across those 'who have just gained the merit of obtaining the title Tulku. Just by force of merit'. Both these latter two types of trulku must have great merit (the result of good deeds in previous lives), since being recognized as a trulku is usually highly advantageous in material terms. Put frankly, trulkus in Tibetan Buddhism are usually relatively wealthy and socially privileged. Such advantages are seen in Buddhism as flowing precisely from merit, the results of one's good deeds in previous lives. But, Doboom Tulku continues, the difference between these two categories is that while those of the third class have accrued sufficient merit to be recognized as trulkus, they may not have the power actually to control the process of rebirth at all. It is to this third category that Doboom Tulku considers he himself belongs, although he adds that because of merit he has obtained the title of 'trulku' and so can use the opportunities this affords him in order to help others. Interestingly Doboom Tulku also observes that he could scarcely claim to be an emanation of a Buddha or a bodhisattva, since he knows who he is. The implication of this is that if one were to be such an emanation, one would know it.[20] We shall see, however, that this specifically contradicts comments made by other Tibetan teachers regarding the possibility of not knowing that one is an emanation.

One corollary of Doboom Tulku's observations is that the trulku of the third category could still be considered by Buddhists a genuine reincarnation, although the teacher who reincarnated obviously had not managed to gain control of his rebirths and therefore was perhaps not as advanced in meditative ability as some considered him to be. But nevertheless this third category may contain within it those whose previous merit had gained the title 'trulku' but who are not, even for Buddhists, actually or genuinely the reincarnations of those they are said to be. In other words, in the issue of discovering a correct reincarnation there had been a mistake. The Dalai Lama recognizes that mistakes do occur. He has estimated that it is quite possible that as many as 50 per cent were mistaken identifications. He adds that he may be quite presumptuous in saying this, but he bases his estimate partly on whether the correct tests were carried out (such as correctly selecting unmarked objects belonging to the previous incarnation, or saying something that indicated intimate knowledge of the previous incarnation's life). Also, it depends on whether the putative trulku genuinely serves humanity or not ('by their fruits ye shall know them').[21]

One should note, however, that from the Tibetan point of view the ability to control the rebirth process is a technique gained through meditation and does not *in itself* entail a measure of what we in the West might call 'spirituality', or 'righteousness'. Thus it is held to be quite possible as a result of developed meditative ability in previous lives to control the rebirth process. One might thus be recognized as a genuine trulku, and yet still (*pace* the Dalai Lama's pious hopes) fritter away one's life and be of no benefit to anyone. This can occur even if in the previous life the trulku was a righteous person who benefited others immensely. It might be lamentable from the Dalai Lama's point of view, but it is still considered possible. Indeed Song Rinpoche has observed that there are those who are reborn and recognized as trulkus who can genuinely control their rebirths, although they took rebirth not in order to help others but out of attachment to their status, property and so on. Not to mention the deceit and pretence that Song Rinpoche holds has sometimes taken place with ordinary children who cannot control their rebirths but are manipulated into a spurious 'recognition' as a result of the riches, possessions and status involved.[22]

Modesty will frequently incline those who are acclaimed as trulkus to assert that they are actually of this last category. This is particularly so as they invariably say (as does the Dalai Lama) that they cannot remember their past lives. On the other hand they will often add that they must have had great merit to be declared trulkus, and they can use the opportunities thus given to them in order to help others.[23] Of course this, from the Dalai Lama's perspective, suggests that they might be genuine trulkus after all.

It is noticeable reading interviews with contemporary trulkus that, faced perhaps with the doubts of the modern world, their inability to remember their previous lives does seem to give some trulkus very real uncertainty. One particularly critical lama, Rakra

Tulku, has claimed that real trulkus should always be able to remember some past lives.[24] Many, including the Dalai Lama, would not agree. Rakra Tulku frankly admits that he does not like the trulku system. He refers to a case where the reincarnation of a teacher was supposedly discovered among the Tibetan refugee community in India, only to find subsequently that the teacher was still alive in Tibet. Tibetan 'Buddhalogians', like their brothers the theologians, are quite capable of explaining away such awkward data.[25]

Some find the problem of memory more acute than others do. The traditional Tibetan view is that there certainly are meditation practices which, if carried out systematically, can lead anyone (not just a Buddhist) to recollect their previous lives. These practices are commonly said to be rather insignificant, in themselves not of great benefit to others, but they are available for the curious (or those who can otherwise think of a use for such an ability). Gonsar Tulku has expressed a rather more optimistic view on the absence of memory. He says that he cannot claim to be anyone very great, but others have given him the position of Gonsar Tulku and he has no particular reason to doubt their estimate. By now it has become part of him. The role has become the actuality.[26] Anyway, for Tibetans, as another trulku, Dakpo Tulku, has pointed out, one cannot tell from the outside who is genuine and who is not.[27] Really, without carrying out the appropriate practices one cannot tell from the inside either.[28]

Once declared and accepted, all putative trulkus tend to be treated as genuine, for it would be rather unwise to treat as false something that is as a matter of fact true. And from a Buddhist point of view even the trulku's behaviour may be no guide to authenticity. One with the far-seeing eyes of a trulku could discern what might seem to be wrong, from the spiritually backward point of view of an ordinary person, as correct and proper.

The Dalai Lama is held to be the reincarnation of the previous Dalai Lama, taking on rebirth out of compassion for others, particularly the Tibetan people. There have to date been 14 Dalai Lamas, that is, recognized trulkus in the Dalai Lama series. The first was a pupil of the great founder of the Dalai Lama's dGe lugs pa tradition in the fifteenth century, although the first actually to be called 'Dalai

Lama' was the third, bSod nams rgya mtsho (pronounced 'Sir nam gya tso' (1543–88)).[29] *Dalai* means ocean, and is the Mongolian equivalent of the Tibetan *rgya mtsho* that has normally been part of the names of the Dalai Lamas. When the Third Dalai Lama converted the Mongolian Altan Khan to his own brand of Buddhism, the Mongolian–Tibetan hybrid title 'Dalai Lama' was bestowed by the Mongolian upon bSod nams rgya mtsho, who then in turn bestowed it retrospectively on his two previous recognized incarnations.

In the case of the Dalai Lama, however, the situation appears to be complicated. Normally, from a Buddhist point of view, a reborn being involves a stage of the same consciousness *continuum* as the person who died, but properly speaking is emphatically not thought to be the same *person*. There is no unchanging substratum – no Self or soul in that sense. Rather, if we imagine the flow of consciousness, 'experiences', as like a river, the reincarnation is a later stage in the overall flow of the river. The later stage *depends* on the former stage – there is a continuum present – but it is not the *same* stage. That stage has passed. So when Dakpo Tulku says in an interview that he doubts he is the same consciousness (continuum) as the previous Dakpo Tulku,[30] he would normally be taken by educated Buddhists as saying that he doubts he is the genuine reincarnation of the previous Dakpo Tulku. Thus the consciousnesses of all the Dalai Lamas should form parts of one consciousness continuum. Unfortunately the present Dalai Lama has said in another context that '[t]his does not mean that all the previous Dalai Lamas have had one continuous consciousness'.[31] I confess that short of asking the Dalai Lama what he means here, it is difficult to know how to take it. In context he is speaking of the Dalai Lamas also being recognized as 'emanations' (*sprul pa-s*) of the very advanced bodhisattva (or, commonly for Tibetans, already a Buddha) Avalokiteśvara. The easiest way to take what he is saying is that while all the Dalai Lamas have been in some sense 'emanations' of Avalokiteśvara, in spite of what is usually thought they have not in fact formed a single reincarnation series.

It is in this context that the controversial figure of the Sixth Dalai Lama may be relevant. As we shall see, the Sixth Dalai Lama returned his monk's vows and preferred to get drunk with his friends, have sex with Lhasa women and take part in archery competitions. In the light of the suggested strategy, one could say that while the Sixth Dalai Lama was a genuine 'emanation' of Avalokiteś-vara acting for the benefit (in some way) of others, he was nevertheless not the reincarnation of the politically strong and forceful Fifth Dalai Lama. The 'Great Fifth' (1617–82) was the first Dalai Lama to rule Tibet, and the one who is said to have discovered that the Dalai Lama series is also a series of 'emanations' of Avalo-kiteśvara.[32] The present Dalai Lama has claimed of the Sixth that 'he was spiritually pre-eminent, but politically, he was weak and disinterested. He could not follow the Fifth Dalai Lama's path. This was a great failure.'[33] But elsewhere the Dalai Lama seems to have said categorically that the Sixth was indeed the true reincarnation of the Fifth, as the State Oracle asserted at the time.[34]

An alternative interpretation of the Dalai Lamas not forming one consciousness continuum might involve the phenomenon of 'split incarnations'. Tibetans tend to agree that very advanced bodhisattvas are capable of reincarnating in more than one form at the same time.[35] The Dalai Lama has stated that there are indications that the Second Dalai Lama (b. 1475) had hundreds of reincarnations: 'Of these there was one outstanding one, who took the name Dalai Lama; the rest went out into the world to be benevolent.'[36] If, for example, the Fourth Dalai Lama (d. 1616), who was a Mongolian and not an ethnic Tibetan, was actually the reincarnation of one of those others he would be a genuine reincarnation of the Second Dalai Lama, inasmuch as he would have the same consciousness continuum as the Second Dalai Lama. But he need not have the same consciousness continuum as the Third Dalai Lama, who would in turn also be a genuine reincarnation of the Second and have the same consciousness continuum as him. This is pure speculation, of course, and it would still not make the Fourth Dalai Lama in this example a reincarnation of the Third in any straightforward sense. But then, nothing here seems very straightforward.

We have looked so far at what might be called the 'horizontal' dimension of the Dalai Lama's being. That is, we have examined his position as part of a trulku series with the previous Dalai Lamas. As a trulku the Dalai Lama is simply the most eminent member of a not infrequent Tibetan religious institution. But he also has a 'vertical' relationship to the bodhisattva (or Buddha) Avalokiteśvara. The Dalai Lama is held to be a *sprul pa* ('trulba'), and this is usually seen as an 'emanation'. Such an emanation is a much rarer phenomenon in Tibetan Buddhism. It is this trulba status that is behind the confused claim that the Dalai Lama is a 'god on earth'. But can we gain a more precise idea of what is considered to be his *actual* relationship with Avalokiteśvara?

The traditional Tibetan view of the Dalai Lama has been clearly expressed by Jigdal Sakya Rinpoche, a trulku of another Tibetan tradition, that of the Sa skya. He states that while the Dalai Lama appears to be merely a simple monk, a person with 'clear vision' can see that he or she is in the presence of Avalokiteśvara himself.[37] In the view of Jigdal Sakya Rinpoche, therefore, the Dalai Lama's relationship to Avalokiteśvara seems to be one of identity. The difference between the Dalai Lama and Avalokiteśvara is simply a difference seen from the side of the perceiver.

The current Dalai Lama has stated that while he is held to be the reincarnation of the previous Dalai Lamas, and believed to be a manifestation of Avalokiteśvara, it is not easy to say whether he truly believes this:

> But as a fifty-six year old, when I consider my experiences during this present life, and given my Buddhist beliefs, I have no difficulty accepting that I am spiritually connected both to the thirteen previous Dalai Lamas, to Chenrezig [the Tibetan name for Avalokiteśvara] and to the Buddha himself.[38]

A 'spiritual connection' seems a rather weaker claim than one of emanation or manifestation, let alone one of identity.

I confess to finding the notion of an 'emanation' vague in the extreme. In the Indian origins of the notion there is often a close connection between the idea of emanation and that of a created similitude or illusory being manifested for some purpose or another by one with great magical ('yogic') power. This idea is conveyed both by the original Sanskrit *nirmāṇakāya* and the literal meaning of the Tibetan expression *sprul sku* ('trulku'). Yet in the Tibetan context manifestations or emanations seem to take on a quasi-independent reality. Song Rinpoche talks of 200 or more emanations (*sprul pa*/trulba) of a particular great teacher, but even the emanator himself might not know all his emanations. Even to discover the 200, we are told, took this particular teacher some time. He did not have immediate awareness. Moreover at least some of the emanations did not know about their status as emanations.[39] The implication is clearly that emanations here can have self-consciousness and are not in any significant sense less *real* than the emanator.

This appears to contrast rather with the idea we get from the Indian yogic tradition. Nevertheless it does seem that the emanator is responsible in some sense for their existence, and is emanating them for a particular purpose. The present Dalai Lama has spoken of emanations that do have a sense of 'I' and those that do not. For example, a bodhisattva like Avalokiteśvara could emanate himself in some form or another. That emanation would be a person, with a sense of 'I'. The emanation might then emanate further emanations. These further emanations could appear to be persons and perform all the functions of persons, he says, but actually there would be only one person – the emanator. He confesses this all sounds a bit like science fiction.[40] The Dalai Lama himself is very fond of describing himself as 'just an ordinary Buddhist monk'. Or, as he puts it at one point, '[w]hatever other people ... may think of me ... from my own point of view I am only a drifter along the way, and I still have a lot to do.'[41]

Clearly, any concept of an emanation that allows the emanation to have an independent reality, independence of action, self-consciousness and, in the case of the Dalai Lamas, to reincarnate in a reincarnation lineage is not what we normally think of as an emanation. On the other hand there are cases where Tibetans are willing to refer to someone as a 'manifestation of a Buddha' because his actions *resemble* those of an incarnation of a Buddha.[42] So it seems that to be considered a manifestation of a Buddha does not necessarily entail that one actually is a Buddha or, for example, an 'occult eject' from a Buddha.

What we want is a clearer idea of what exactly is meant by referring to the Dalai Lamas as 'emanations'. Fortunately the present

Dalai Lama has occasionally made reference to what seems to me to be a much more satisfactory and realistic idea of what is being claimed in saying that the Dalai Lama is an 'emanation' of Avalokiteśvara.

I mentioned earlier that the Dalai Lama has spoken of four types of rebirth or incarnation. The first is ordinary uncontrolled rebirth. The second is that of trulkus who are capable of controlling in some way their rebirths. The Dalai Lama goes on to speak of:

(C) '[A]n entirely enlightened Buddha, who simply manifests a physical form to help others. In this case it is clear that the person is a Buddha'.

While it seems certain that this is indeed how Tibetans see the Dalai Lama, it is difficult to square this with his also being part of a horizontal series of reincarnations. Such a manifested physical form is not the *reincarnation* of anyone. It is a manifestation of a physical form. It is also difficult to square it with those who do not clearly see him as a Buddha. Moreover there are the Dalai Lama's own claims that previous Dalai Lamas made mistakes, and that while Tibetans consider him to be a Buddha, even omniscient, he is just an ordinary monk with still far to go on the path – presumably the path to full Buddhahood.

But there is another alternative. The Dalai Lama has also spoken of a fourth type of incarnation:

(D) '[That is] a blessed manifestation. In this the person is blessed beyond his normal capacity to perform helpful functions, such as teaching religion. For this last type of birth, the person's wishes in previous lives to help others must have been very strong. They then obtain such empowerment.'[43]

The Dalai Lama has observed that it is not clear which type of incarnation he is, although some seem more likely than others. I am inclined to think that he must favour this fourth option, and even within Buddhist doctrinal terms this seems a more realistic possibility. More recently he has observed that 'we' (presumably Tibetans) believe that the Dalai Lamas 'were specially blessed by Avalokiteś-vara' and are *therefore* regarded as the reincarnations of

Avalokiteśvara.[44] In a meditation practice written at the age of 19 for other Tibetans, the Dalai Lama subscribes to the traditional view of himself as Avalokiteśvara in the form of one wearing the robes of a monk. But by the time of his first autobiography he describes himself in the context of the possibility of being killed by the Chinese as 'only a mortal being and the instrument of the never-dying spirit of my Master'.[45] If the Dalai Lama were simply identical with Avalokiteśvara, or even an emanation in any normal sense of the word 'emanation', it would not be possible to kill him.[46] Emanations are simply withdrawn by their emanator, not killed.

This idea of the Dalai Lama as a representative, or even a servant, of Avalokiteśvara fits in with the fourth type of incarnation, a blessed manifestation, a person blessed by Avalokiteśvara due to that person's previous vows of great compassion. Elsewhere the Dalai Lama has spoken directly of his own incarnation as blessed by Avalokiteśvara. He also speaks of having 'received the blessing', and being sent to earth as the representative of Avalokiteśvara. But he adds that he prefers to think of himself as just a monk.[47] Thus my suggestion is that the balance of possibility indicates that in Buddhist terms the Dalai Lamas are what is known as 'blessed manifestations' rather than direct emanations or manifestations of Avalokiteśvara in the sense in which emanations (nirmāṇakāya-s) are normally referred to in Indian Buddhism. And I also suggest that the present Dalai Lama himself veers towards this interpretation. Moreover I do not think this is a new way of seeing the Dalai Lamas. I would imagine that apart from feelings of great reverence and devotion by ordinary Tibetans, who would be inclined to see the Dalai Lama as simply and literally a Buddha, doctrinally, inasmuch as there has been reflection on the subject, the Dalai Lamas have always been thought of as blessed manifestations. They are human beings blessed beyond their normal capacities by Avalokiteśvara. This blessing is granted to them through their cultivation over many lifetimes of immense compassion.

I have referred already to the problematic case of the Sixth Dalai Lama. I shall return in the next section to the life and times of the Sixth. But it seems difficult to avoid the view that this Dalai Lama's own disinclination to be involved with either the Tibetan ecclesias-

tical or political structures of his day contributed to Tibet falling
victim both to rival Mongolian clans and also to the machinations of
the Manchu Chinese emperor. When the Sixth Dalai Lama was
captured by an occupying force of the Mongolian Lha bzang Khan,
an attempt was made to have him deposed by his own people. A
group of abbots was eventually persuaded under Mongolian pressure
to announce that the *byang chub* (pronounced 'jang chup') of Avalo-
kiteśvara had left the Dalai Lama.[48] It is clear from this that the
Dalai Lama was not even then seen as literally *being* Avalokiteśvara.
Rather, he is one on whom something of Avalokiteśvara had
descended. *Byang chub* is the Tibetan translation of the Sanskrit
bodhi, enlightenment. It comes from the same Sanskrit root as the
word *Buddha*. But the abbots could not have been intending to say
that enlightenment, even the enlightenment of Avalokiteśvara, had
left the Dalai Lama. Enlightenment, once possessed, cannot be lost
and the enlightenment of one being cannot be transferred to
another. Thus, I suggest, *byang chub* here means not enlightenment
at all. It is rather a typical Tibetan shortening of either *byang chub
sems dpa'* (pronounced 'jang chup sem pa', i.e. bodhisattva), or *byang
chub sems* (pronounced 'jang chup sem', i.e. bodhicitta, the awakening
mind). Thus what the abbots were trying to say was that either the
bodhisattva, Avalokiteśvara, had left the Sixth Dalai Lama – which is
to say that Avalokiteśvara had withdrawn his blessing – or that the
awakening mind had been lost. The awakening mind must in this
context mean the great compassion that had led to Avalokiteśvara's
supreme blessing. The Sixth Dalai Lama had shown by his behav-
iour that he no longer had that great compassion for others. Either
way the Dalai Lama no longer had the blessing of Avalokiteśvara. If
the Dalai Lama was seen simply as Avalokiteśvara in a monk's guise,
or an 'emanation' in the normal sense of the word, it would not be
possible for the Dalai Lama to remain in existence having lost his
connection with Avalokiteśvara.

I want now to summarize what I have said in this lengthy section.
Who or what *is* the Dalai Lama?

1. In worldly terms, a Dalai Lama is a Buddhist monk. He is a monk
– indeed usually an abbot – of the dGe lugs pa (the 'Virtuous Ones',

9

the Goodies) tradition of Tibetan Buddhism. This is a tradition (associated with yellow hats) that makes a virtue of Virtue. The Dalai Lama may also be a learned monk. He is at least expected or hoped to be spiritually reasonably adept. Thus the unexpected behaviour of the Sixth Dalai Lama, and his decision to return his monastic vows, faced his fellow Buddhists with an unexpected challenge and threat. In defence of the Sixth Dalai Lama, however, while monks dominate Tibetan Buddhism, there also exist lay spiritual teachers. In particular tantric practices within Tibetan Buddhism, which involve at advanced levels the practitioner taking a consort for ritual practice, might provide a model for neutralizing criticism of the sexual involvement of the Sixth. This lay model is, however, associated mainly with other non-dGe lugs traditions of Tibetan Buddhism. It would have found little sympathy among most in the dGe lugs hierarchy.

2. From the seventeenth century the Dalai Lamas have also been, at least in theory and providing they reached their majority, heads of the Tibetan state. Therefore the behaviour of the Sixth Dalai Lama, coming so soon after the establishment of the Dalai Lamas as heads of state at the time of the Fifth Dalai Lama, was a matter of political as well as religious importance. Tantric practice or not, many would have considered the Sixth needed to remain an orthodox dGe lugs monk-practitioner in order to encourage stability and not to rock the boat of state.

3. The Dalai Lamas are also held to be advanced Mahāyāna bodhisattvas. Thus they are thought to be well on the way to Buddhahood, developing perfection in wisdom and compassion for the benefit of all sentient beings. It is this bodhisattva status of the Dalai Lama that justifies doctrinally his willingness to engage in the dirty life of politics in order to help others. On the other hand since an advanced bodhisattva is considered to be working to help others in ways that might not be immediately obvious to 'ordinary mortals', this status of the Sixth Dalai Lama should have helped to ameliorate any unrestrained criticism by others of his conduct.

4. A Dalai Lama is also a *sprul sku* (trulku). We have seen that in its Indian Buddhist origins this term refers to an emanation – or a 'transformation' – body manifested by a Buddha in order to help ordinary sentient beings. In Tibetan Buddhism, however, the expression has come to be used to refer to a person who is considered to be a reincarnation of an identified previous teacher. The normal implication is that the previous teacher developed the ability through spiritual cultivation to control his or her rebirths in order to return to continue (it is hoped) the bodhisattva path of helping others. Thus it happens that a child is identified as the reincarnation and trained to re-adopt his or her previous position and status. The trulkus form an important institution in the Tibetan Buddhist hierarchy, providing in particular a degree of 'hereditary' continuity within a political system that came to be dominated by celibate monks. On the other hand we have also seen that Tibetans do not necessarily hold that just because someone is a trulku they will behave virtuously. Behaviour in this life for good or evil is still an open question. Thus among those who would criticize the Sixth Dalai Lama, his trulku status would not *as such* entail a limit to criticism. There have been a number of other cases in Tibetan Buddhism where trulkus have been subject to severe censure.

5. Finally, the Dalai Lama is also a *sprul pa* (trulba). This is a much rarer phenomenon in Tibetan Buddhism. Tibetans normally speak of a trulba as an emanation of an important named 'transcendental' bodhisattva. Thus since the seventeenth century the Dalai Lamas have been considered to be trulbas of the bodhisattva of compassion, Avalokiteśvara. We have seen that this trulba status can entail seeing the Dalai Lama as literally Avalokiteśvara in person, in the form of a human monk. However, I have argued that the present Dalai Lama would incline towards a less exalted estimation of his status, and there is evidence in Tibetan doctrinal history to support this. Thus the Dalai Lama as a trulba is someone who has been blessed by Avalokiteśvara as the result of the former's strong vows of compassion in previous lives. A Dalai Lama is thereby enabled to act compassionately beyond his normal human capacity. Since to be a trulba involves being the recipient of a particular blessing or

empowerment, it therefore becomes possible to argue that the recipient needs by his or her acts to justify continued possession of the blessing. In the case of the Sixth Dalai Lama, it could be claimed, his conduct meant or entailed that Avalokiteśvara could withdraw his blessing. Thus a Dalai Lama could lose his status as a trulba. The claim by a group of abbots (albeit apparently under Mongolian pressure) that Avalokiteśvara had indeed withdrawn his blessing from the Sixth Dalai Lama failed. I suggest it failed precisely because most Tibetans had in practice come to see the Dalai Lama as actually being Avalokiteśvara in person. This exalted status (compare the 'divine right of kings' in Western political theory) was clearly in the interests of a strong Dalai Lama like the Fifth in securing his control over the Tibetan state. Once a Dalai Lama is seen as actually being Avalokiteśvara, the Dalai Lama's status as an advanced compassionate bodhisattva beyond criticism by ordinary mortals becomes enhanced. Thus can criticism and control by others be offset.

6. We should also note here two things a Dalai Lama is *not*. First he is not in any simple sense a 'god-king'. He may be a sort of king, but he is not for Buddhism a god. Second, in spite of what is often said, the Dalai Lama is not 'the Head (or 'Pope') of Tibetan Buddhism', let alone of Buddhism as a whole. There are many traditions of Buddhism. Some have nominated 'Heads', some do not. Within Tibet too there are a number of traditions. Because of his political significance, and also often his spiritual distinction, the Dalai Lama will usually be given enormous respect. But he is not the Head of all, or each of, the Tibetan Buddhist traditions. Indeed he is not even Head of his own dGe lugs tradition. The Head of the dGe lugs is whoever is abbot of dGa' ldan (pronounced 'Ganden') monastery, in succession to Tsong kha pa, the dGe lugs founder. In recent centuries this has not been the Dalai Lama.

The attempt by the abbots to depose the Sixth Dalai Lama, to ruin Tibetan faith in their Dalai Lama, failed. But to see why let us now turn to the life and times of this extraordinary and extraordinarily tragic figure.

The life and times of the Sixth Dalai Lama

As we have seen, the Dalai Lamas are institutionally members of the dGe lugs pa tradition of Tibetan Buddhism. The Sixth Dalai Lama, however, was born in 1683 into a family with hereditary associations with another Tibetan tradition, that known as 'The Ancient Ones' (or 'The Old Translation School'), the rNying ma pa (pronounced 'Nyingmapa'). This was not unusual. The Fifth Dalai Lama too had associations with the rNying ma pa by birth and by inclination in his personal meditation practice. Nevertheless, while this might show a broad measure of doctrinal tolerance within Tibetan Buddhism at that time, politically Tibet then was far from tolerant. In the words of Sir Charles Bell, who knew Tibet well from first-hand experience, 'There was no tolerance at that time [the seventeenth century]; battles were fought and monasteries were pillaged.'[49] The monasteries, and thus their traditions of Buddhism, were closely involved in political rivalry. They had been so since at least the time of the great Mongol expansion in the thirteenth century. Faced in Tibet with large powerful monasteries, but by this time a weak secular rulership, the Mongol Khan chose to control Tibet by simply giving Tibet to the most respected Tibetan lama of the day, and backing him up if necessary with fierce and ruthless Mongol armies. This was formalized and consolidated when the Mongols under Kublai Khan (d. 1295) completed their conquest of China. The gift was understood by Tibetans (in accordance with an old Indian model of the relationship between a king and his chief priest) to be a recognition on the part of the Khan that the lama stands in an ultimately superior position to the Khan. The lama is his spiritual teacher (his guru). Hence he is the superior partner just as the spiritual realm is superior to the world. The Khan was in effect the lay patron, the lama his royal priest, and Tibet the offering made by the disciple to his teacher.

The first school of Tibetan Buddhism to control Tibet politically was the Sa skya school, led by the revered Sa skya Paṇḍita (1182–1251). This school was named after its principal monastery of Sa skya (pronounced 'Sagya' – 'Grey Earth') in southern Tibet. Under the Mongols the Sa skya school of Tibetan Buddhism also had enormous influence at the very centres of imperial power in

China. With the collapse of Mongol control in China (known there as the Yüan dynasty) and the accession of the indigenous Han Chinese empire of the Ming (1368–1644), Sa skya dominance of Tibet also waned. But in Tibet the model and ideal of rule by monasteries continued. Moreover, even though the Mongols no longer controlled China and Mongol power had fragmented into a number of rival warring clans, the Mongols were still militarily a powerful force in Central Asia. The need to control them and ideally keep the Mongols disunited was a major foreign policy concern of successive Chinese Ming emperors. And the Mongols, with their Khans, were for many centuries to come still among the principal powerbrokers in Tibet.

The dGe lugs tradition emerged right at the beginning of the fifteenth century in partial reaction against the inevitable corruption that went with the political involvement of monks and monasteries. The very name *dGe lugs pa* means 'the Goodies', the Virtuous Ones. In fact the dGe lugs pas were so good, both in virtue and in learning, that the dGe lugs tradition proved extremely attractive, and it prospered. By 1560, when the Third Dalai Lama (d. 1588) stepped in to bring to an end fighting in Lhasa between rival enthusiasts for the bKa' brgyud (pronounced 'Kagyer') tradition and for the dGe lugs, the dGe lugs was already becoming itself a major player in Tibetan politics. The Third was the first to be called 'Dalai Lama', and was responsible for finally converting many of the Mongol tribes to his dGe lugs brand of Tibetan Buddhism. With widespread and powerful Mongol allegiance to the dGe lugs cause from that time on, dGe lugs secular power was set to increase. Eventually, under the Fifth Dalai Lama, it led to the whole of Tibet resting in dGe lugs hands.

We can see then that the Tibetan Buddhist traditions showed a political intolerance that belied their broad (but by no means total) doctrinal tolerance. Thus (to take just one example) in 1618 the chief of Tsang (*gTsang*), the large province in southern Tibet, attacked the great dGe lugs pa monasteries of Drepung ('*Bras spungs*) and Sera. The Tsang chief was allied to another tradition of Tibetan Buddhism, the Karma sub-school of the bKa' brgyud, that had become very powerful throughout Tibet but particularly in the

south. The dGe lugs monasteries (together with a third, Ganden
(*dGa' ldan*)) dominated the Lhasa region. The Tsang chief attacked
them after meeting armed resistance from the dGe lugs monks to a
raid he was making on Lhasa. Many monks were killed. Some small
dGe lugs monasteries were forcibly converted to bKa' brgyud. The
chief of Tsang also founded a monastery of his own called Trashi
Zilnon (*bKra shis zil non*), the 'Suppressor of Trashi', referring to the
great dGe lugs pa monastery of Trashi Hlunbo (*bKra shis lhun po*) in
southern Tibet, which it overlooked. In building this monastery,
stones were rolled down from the mountain side on to the dGe lugs
monks below, killing several of them. The aggression was not all one
way. The reason for the chief of Tsang to attack at this time was
what was felt to be insulting and disparaging treatment of him by the
attendants of the Fourth Dalai Lama (d. 1617). Even earlier, at the
turn of the seventeenth century, Mongol horsemen attached to the
Fourth Dalai Lama, who was himself ethnically a Mongol, attacked
Karma bKa' brgyud housing and stables. This in turn led to what
had been an earlier raid on Lhasa by the soldiers from Tsang (1605).
Perhaps much of the aggression between Tsang, dominated by the
bKa' brgyud schools, and the central province (*dBus*, pronounced 'Ü')
around Lhasa, under the control of the dGe lugs and their allies,
reflected age-old rivalries. This was between central Tibet with its
capital of Lhasa, and the prosperous south of the country, on the
borders of India and Nepal. Lhasa was the old capital of the almost
legendary Tibetan emperors of the seventh to ninth centuries. And
in spite of frequent rivalry and fighting between monasteries, monks
and their lay partisans, great lamas sometimes stepped in to mediate
and defuse aggression between armies.

I do not want to dwell at length on how the 'Great Fifth' Dalai
Lama eventually came to rule the whole of Tibet. It is sometimes
said that his takeover was motivated by a wisdom and compassion
that realized Tibet would never be at peace until ruled by one man,
himself. But in his own autobiographical account he states that he
did not initiate the move towards political dominance and power. As
a Buddhist monk, the Dalai Lama wanted to avoid bloodshed – or at
least being thought responsible for more bloodshed than was strictly
necessary under the circumstances. It was the Dalai Lama's chief

attendant who pushed him into a corner where the only course was to sanction the complete destruction of the then ruling 'Regent' of Tsang and his Karma bKa' brgyud religious allies. It happened like this.

Faced with an alliance between Tsang, some Mongol supporters and a king from Eastern Tibet, aimed as far as he could tell at completely destroying the dGe lugs school once and for all, the Fifth Dalai Lama appealed for military support from his Mongol devotees under the powerful Gushri Khan. According to his own account, the Dalai Lama would have been happy with the defeat of the eastern king, and he did not ask for Gushri Khan to destroy Tsang as well. But orally the Dalai Lama's chief attendant suggested to the Khan that, having defeated the former, Gushri Khan should complete the task and remove the Regent of Tsang too.[50] This eventually happened. Even the Dalai Lama came to agree that matters had gone too far for them to step back from this final confrontation. Gushri Khan defeated and captured the Regent of Tsang. With the complete defeat of the main rivals to dGe lugs power, Gushri Khan himself was now nominally King of Tibet. But, on the model supplied by the great earlier Mongol Khans, in 1642 Gushri Khan gave control of Tibet over to the Fifth Dalai Lama. With a subsequent bKa' brgyud revolt crushed, Gushri Khan had the Tsang Regent executed. The Dalai Lama, backed if necessary by powerful Mongol forces, now for the first time controlled all of Tibet.

The sheer importance of the Dalai Lama in Tibet and Mongol-dominated Central Asia was underlined by an invitation for him to visit the Chinese emperor. In 1644 the Chinese Ming empire finally collapsed. It was overthrown by the Manchus, from north-eastern China. The Manchus founded the Ch'ing Dynasty that was to remain the imperial dynasty in China until 1911. Similar in ethnic and cultural origin to the Mongols, the Manchus knew only too well the danger that could be posed by Mongols and in particular Mongol unity. Accordingly they valued Tibet under a strong Dalai Lama who had direct control over the Mongol clans. For Chinese foreign policy the Dalai Lama himself – the actual person of the Dalai Lama with the spiritual significance and prestige that went with it – was central to their plans for controlling and defusing Mongol military strength. Through his religious significance for the Mongols, the Dalai Lama was to be the means by which the emperor in Beijing could control if necessary, or divide and rule if need be, the dangerous Mongol warlords.[51] This is important if we are to understand the political disaster for Mongols and Chinese (not to mention for Tibetans) of the Sixth Dalai Lama's lack of interest in his role as Dalai Lama.

The Fifth Dalai Lama was a tireless, energetic and by all accounts relatively tolerant ruler. The period of his rule is often thought of as being a golden age for Tibet. He strictly controlled those traditions of Tibetan Buddhism, such as the Karma bKa' brgyud, that had provided focuses of opposition to the establishment of dGe lugs rule. Some monasteries were forcibly converted to the dGe lugs, and one tradition of Tibetan Buddhism, the Jo nang pa, was suppressed. But otherwise the Great Fifth let traditions be traditions, and employed in government service lamas from traditions other than dGe lugs. He himself rather favoured the rNying ma pa teachings, and among the many works he wrote on Buddhist doctrine, history, poetry and goodness knows what else, there were works written within the rNying ma rather than the dGe lugs religious ethos. The Fifth toured Tibet, and together with a series of regents he established the political system that largely remained until the 1950s. As a ruler, albeit a Buddhist monk, he certainly had no problem with the necessities of judicial execution and war. He himself commented in one of his works that 'no pity should be wasted on a man who had to be executed for his crimes'.[52] Waging aggressive war was by no means beyond him if he felt it was necessary. A number of times during his rule Tibetan armies invaded the little Himalayan kingdom of Bhutan, and each time they were defeated. The Great Fifth was not always successful in his enterprises. To the present day Bhutan remains under the dominance of a bKa' brgyud sub-school. Johannes Grueber, an Austrian Jesuit who visited Lhasa at the time, spoke of the Fifth Dalai Lama as the 'devilish God-the-Father who puts to death such as refuse to adore him'.[53] But it has to be said that Grueber was hardly an objective judge. Shakabpa, a former Tibetan civil servant, comments in his political history of Tibet that:

Politically, the fifth Dalai Lama was very successful in unifying the country. Previously, there had been constant struggle for power between different religious sects, ruling families, and powerful chiefs. The Dalai Lama succeeded in winning the allegiance of the chieftains within Tibet as well as those on the border. Taxation was just and no exemptions were made. Although he was sympathetic in dealing with his subjects, he could be ruthless in stamping out rebellion.[54]

As we saw previously, it was the Fifth Dalai Lama who discerned that as well as a 'horizontal' relationship of rebirth to the previous Dalai Lamas, the Dalai Lama also possesses a 'vertical' relationship, a special relationship, to the bodhisattva Avalokiteśvara. And it was no doubt in accordance with this relationship that he commenced the building of the vast palace, the Potala, towering over the city of Lhasa. The name 'Potala' comes from the supposed home of Avalokiteśvara, said to be somewhere in southern India. The actual mountain in Lhasa where the Potala was built was the site of the ruins of the palace of the ancient Tibetan kings. By the time of the Fifth it was already thought that the first of the great Tibetan emperors, Srong btsan sgam po (pronounced 'Songtsen Gambo'; d. 649) was a direct manifestation of Avalokiteśvara. Avalokiteśvara was a bodhisattva who, while compassionate for all, had a particular care and concern for Tibet and Tibetans. Now he was (as it were) to live there in the Potala, in Lhasa, the centre of the Tibetan world, in the middle of the *mandala*, in the person of the Dalai Lama himself.

Gushri Khan died in 1655. The Fifth Dalai Lama himself died in 1682, aged 68. He died well before the completion of the Potala Palace. As a Buddhist monk and scholar, as well as a ruler, he had been ably served by a series of chief ministers. These ministers were known as 'regents' (*sde srid*; pronounced 'desi'). The most important of them, and the one in power at the time of the Dalai Lama's death, was Desi Sangyay Gyatso (Tibetan: sDe srid Sangs rgyas rgya mtsho). Because of the importance of this man to our story, I shall refer to him from now on simply as 'the Regent'.

Like the Dalai Lama himself, the Regent was a formidable scholar and a skilled politician who could also be ruthless when he thought it necessary. It has even been suggested that the Regent was actually the illegitimate son of the Fifth Dalai Lama, although Shakabpa points out that the Fifth himself forced the resignation of a previous regent precisely for breaking his vow of celibacy. So, he argues, it is not very likely that the Dalai Lama did so himself.[55] Among the Regent's writings are some of the most important Tibetan works on medicine and astrology, as well as history. The Regent himself remained throughout his life a layman, and Aris speaks of him as 'the most accomplished lay scholar Tibet ever produced'.[56] He attributes much of this accomplishment to the influence of the Fifth Dalai Lama. The Fifth had brought up Sangyay Gyatso from childhood with the intention that eventually he would become Regent of Tibet.

The Regent was also an enthusiast for (inter alia) archery, poetry, music and folksong. These are pursuits that will reappear in his great discovery, the Sixth Dalai Lama, as will their shared enthusiasm for sex. Along with his two official wives, it is said of the Regent that 'of the noble ladies of Lhasa and those who came there from the provinces, there was not a single one whom the regent did not take [to bed]'.[57]

With the death of the Dalai Lama and the Potala only half completed, the expected next move was for the Regent to commence a search for the reincarnation of the Dalai Lama. He could then begin the long process of education before the Sixth, at a suitable age, could resume full rule of Tibet again. But the Regent did not do this. Instead he announced to the Tibetans that the Dalai Lama was entering religious retreat. No mention was made that the Fifth had actually died. With this explanation the Regent continued to rule the state in the name of the Fifth Dalai Lama, using all the official seals of the Dalai Lama, for some 15 years after the Fifth's death (1682–1697). When distinguished visiting dignitaries had to be granted an audience with the Dalai Lama, a monk bearing some resemblance to the Fifth impersonated him, apparently very unwillingly. At least one case is recorded where the secret leaked out. The Regent had the two people who had discovered the truth murdered.

Why the Regent kept the death of the Fifth Dalai Lama secret for so long is not clear.[58] Uncharitable assessment would have it that the Regent, who had been in power for only three years at the time of the death of the Fifth Dalai Lama, wished to retain political control for as long as possible. But there is nothing to say that he could not have remained in power during the minority of the Sixth Dalai Lama anyway. Loss of power would be no more likely under a minority than under the ever possible risk of discovery.[59] A more charitable judgement is that the Regent genuinely considered that Tibet was too unstable for the death of the Dalai Lama to be announced. Sources refer frequently to the Regent consulting forms of divination such as the Tibetan State Oracle, a monk who, in trance, is possessed by a protector god of Tibet that speaks through him. The Regent no doubt did this in order to determine what to do and whether the time was right to divulge the secret. Often the Oracle expressed concerns, and it would be wrong to think that the Regent did not genuinely accept and heed the words of oracles. Even the present Fourteenth Dalai Lama does. To let it be known at the wrong time that the Great Fifth Dalai Lama was dead could be disastrous. It was the Dalai Lama who held control over the Mongol clans, not anyone else – least of all a regent who initially had been in power for only three years. In particular, it is said that the Regent thought that if the death of the Dalai Lama was known there would no longer be the control and impetus needed to ensure the comple-tion of the vast Potala Palace. According to the Regent himself, the Fifth Dalai Lama made this point as he lay dying. It was confirmed subsequently by consulting the oracles. The symbol of the Potala was central to the Tibetan vision of the Dalai Lamas as Avalokiteśvara present in Lhasa. It was to be the central symbol of the new, stable, benevolent regime, and to manifest the actuality of Avalokiteśvara's concern for Tibet in the person of the Dalai Lamas.

It would be wrong to think that the Regent did not hold dearly to the truth of all this. Nevertheless it is not clear that the Fifth expected or advised secrecy for 15 years. The problems experienced with the Sixth Dalai Lama may well reflect the length of time in which the reincarnation was effectively kept imprisoned before his discovery could be announced to the Tibetan people and his public training as Dalai Lama begin in earnest. This is a point that was recognized by later Tibetan historians themselves. I shall return to it below.

Of course the Regent was perfectly aware that the Fifth Dalai Lama was dead. Thus a search for his reincarnation had to take place, but without arousing wide suspicions about whom it was they were seeking. We know of the early years of the Sixth Dalai Lama from an account written by the Regent himself. In good Tibetan fashion it is replete with divinatory dreams, oracular pronouncements and 'clear signs' of the child selected being the true reincarnation of the Fifth Dalai Lama. The child eventually recognized as the reincarnation was born in 1683 in the region known as Mon (pronounced 'Mern') in the far south of Tibet (see verse 46, and comments). The Fifth Dalai Lama himself had incorporated this region into Tibet proper recently. It is said that this remarkable child's first words were, 'I'm not someone insignificant, but rather Gyalwa Lobsang Gyamtso [i.e. the Fifth Dalai Lama], the Refuge of the Three Worlds.'[60]

The distinguished monks charged with searching for the reincarnation were told to let it be known that they were actually searching for the rebirth of another recently deceased lama. They could not be searching for the Dalai Lama. He was, of course, still alive in retreat in Lhasa. And so it remained, even after selecting the lad from Mon as the true reincarnation. No one was told that he was actually the reincarnation of the long dead Dalai Lama. At the age of two years and eight months the child and his parents were taken from their home to a location two days' journey away. They were then transferred to the district headquarters, another place known as 'Tsona' (mTsho sna). Tsona was described by travellers in the 1930s as 'filthy, wind-swept Tsona', 'a filthy village of close on a hundred hovels hardly fit for human habitation'.[61] There the family was effectively held under house arrest, mainly in one room, and probably in the local fortress. Initially food was poor. They were frequently insulted by the two local governors for reasons that may have had something to do with rivalries within the child's extended family. The very early childhood of the Sixth Dalai Lama was one of imprisonment, abuse, hunger, family bitterness and initially a very real fear that they were going to be killed.

This sense of restriction and imprisonment continued even after the Regent was satisfied through repeated tests (at first, it is said, those involved felt some doubt) that this child was indeed the reincarnation of the Fifth Dalai Lama. Still no one else was told that this was the case. Tsangyang Gyatso's parents did not know until 1696, his 13th year. The local officials in Tsona were told in 1697. But the moment the examiners and the Regent were convinced, the little child was separated from his family, including his mother. Living conditions were improved somewhat, but it is said that the Dalai Lama's parents remained deeply upset by the treatment they had received. They nursed their grievances for a long time. But then at that time they had little choice. Much later, in 1697 soon after the Sixth Dalai Lama had been formally announced, his father died just when he was coming into the riches that go with being a parent of a Dalai Lama. But before he died he himself dictated a list of grievances which the Dalai Lama's mother eventually presented to the Regent. The Regent was shocked at the behaviour over all those years of the two governors of Tsona. They finally met their karmic comeuppance. They were stripped of their offices, their wealth was confiscated and they were reduced to the level of commoners. The Dalai Lama's parents – certainly his mother – were toughies.

It is sometimes claimed that because of the plot to keep the death of the Fifth Dalai Lama secret, the Sixth cannot have been trained properly for his future career as Dalai Lama and this might explain his subsequent behaviour. That is not strictly true. Although he was effectively under house arrest all those years, with very restricted contact with others, Tsangyang Gyatso (as he was later to be known) was given something resembling a respectable education from the age of four. Indeed the nature of his education as described by the Regent in his writing suggested to Aris that the Regent hoped to mould the Sixth Dalai Lama into a little version of the Great Fifth. Since the Regent considered that the Sixth was the reincarnation of the Fifth, he doubtless thought that the Sixth would immediately master ('recollect') the difficult writings of his predecessor and himself, the Regent. Tsangyang Gyatso was expected to be very, very clever. He had everyone of any real significance in his very restricted world looking at him, wanting and expecting signs of cleverness. As Aris puts it in what is by far the most important recent scholarly study of the Sixth Dalai Lama's life:

[I]t would appear from all this that the regent was trying to re-create something of the scholarly atmosphere he had known in his own youth when he had sat at the feet of the Great Fifth, also later when they had together poured forth the most weighty and enduring works of scholarship. Because of the constraints imposed by secrecy and distance, the only way the clock could be turned back to those times was by imposing on the boy the weight of dead letters. The mere recitation of these was supposed to rekindle the spark of learning and wisdom. At no point are we afforded a glimpse of what was really going on in the mind of the young boy. However, it can perhaps be guessed that the efforts to mould him into the form of his predecessor were felt to be just as constraining as the walls of the fortress where he was confined.[62]

It was Manchu pressure that eventually led to the public announcement of the death of the Fifth Dalai Lama and the formal discovery of the Sixth. By now the Chinese Manchu emperor was the powerful K'ang-hsi (1661–1722), without doubt the greatest of all the Ch'ing emperors. He still had problems with the Mongols. Defeating in battle in 1696 one particularly difficult Mongol Khan, K'ang-hsi heard from prisoners rumours of the death of the Fifth Dalai Lama. Investigating, he was less than happy to find that the Regent had concealed the death of the Fifth for so long even from him, the Son of Heaven in Beijing. The Chinese liked to think that all surrounding nations were institutionally dependent on the Chinese emperor. For the Regent to hide a matter of central importance to the state was deeply worrying. The emperor did not forget it.

So the secret was finally out. In his early teens the Sixth Dalai Lama was finally declared and ordained as a novice monk. His teacher and ordination master was the Second Panchen Lama of Trashi Hlunbo Monastery. The first Panchen Lama had been the teacher of the Fifth Dalai Lama. Traditionally whichever is the older incarnation between the Panchen and the Dalai Lamas acts as the teacher to the other. As far as the dGe lugs vision of the Tibetan state is concerned the Panchen Lama ranks next after the Dalai Lama. It was only at this time, the time of his ordination, that the lad was given his official name of 'Tsangyang Gyatso'.[63] But at the time of his novice ordination even the Regent noticed that perhaps not everything was as it should be. 'While having his hair washed just before the ceremony of tonsure the boy broke down weeping. "This auspice," said the regent, "was difficult to understand."'[64]

In 1697, after his ordination, Tsangyang Gyatso was enthroned in Lhasa as the Sixth Dalai Lama. While day-to-day administration was still in the hands of the Regent, the Dalai Lama's life was now one constant round of official duties and education. He was still severely restricted by the personnel, ritual and protocol of the Potala and the Tibetan government. How he felt about using the 'little black seal' to stamp endless boring documents can be seen perhaps in verse 14. But Tsangyang Gyatso, like his mother, was also a toughie. By early 1701 we find the Regent declaring to some leading dGe lugs pa abbots that the Dalai Lama would listen to no one concerning his studies, not even his mother. Aris suggests that a learned work attributed to the Sixth Dalai Lama and written at this time was probably ghosted, and represents the last attempt by the Regent to represent Tsangyang Gyatso as a worthy scholarly successor to the Great Fifth.[65] There is increasing evidence towards the end of the Regent's account that the Dalai Lama was going his own way. He was refusing to do more than the bare minimum required of him. He was becoming uncontrollable. In the modern West those who have had teenage children might be able to recognize the phenomenon.

We are in 1701. The Dalai Lama was in his 19th year. He would soon be expected to take full monk's ordination. But we know from letters initially between the Regent and the Dalai Lama's teacher, the Panchen Lama, and subsequently between the Dalai Lama himself and the Panchen, that matters were not proceeding according to plan. The Dalai Lama went to southern Tibet, to Trashi Hlunbo Monastery, to visit the Panchen Lama in person. He stayed not at the monastery but rather in a mansion house in the neighbouring town. In fact Tsangyang Gyatso refused to sit on the high monastic throne, and refused to do all the religious things expected of him as the great lama, the Sixth Dalai Lama. Most important of all, in spite of entreaties by the Panchen Lama, the Dalai Lama did something that would still be most unexpected of any traditional Tibetan, let alone an incarnate lama. He rejected the requests of his teacher, his guru. Not only would he not take full monastic vows but he also returned even the novice vows he had taken already. From now on the Dalai Lama would be a layman. And have fun. Like the Regent.

Other distinguished lamas too added their voices. Please, please could the Dalai Lama just behave in a way expected of a Dalai Lama? The answer was 'No'! After 17 days Tsangyang Gyatso returned to Lhasa. And even when begged not to dress like a layman, he refused. The Dalai Lama wanted to dress like a layman. One eyewitness describes Tsangyang Gyatso dressed in lay clothes of blue silk, wearing several rings, with long hair, carrying a bow, and devoting scant time to official requests or petitions before rushing off to archery with his attendants and friends.[66] Another eyewitness describes Tsangyang Gyatso surrounded by several distinguished friends and attendants, including at least one incarnate lama. They were all completely drunk, except apparently the Dalai Lama himself, who carried on as if unaffected. He 'gave counsels, wrote compositions and sang songs without error, being not in the least bit altered [by the effect of alcohol]'.[67] But we know from accounts of the twentieth-century 'renegade dGe lugs pa monk' dGe 'dun chos phel (Gendun Cherpel) that the theme of a Tibetan religious hero unaffected by vast amounts of alcohol is not uncommon. The implication is that if alcohol has no affect this is an indication of great *siddhi*, great 'yogic power'. It adds to the sense of otherworldliness in one's hero, a sense that 'there is more here than meets the eye'. But it also suggests not alcoholism perhaps but at least a refined level of tolerance to alcohol that comes with considerable practice.

Once more like so many parents of modern teenagers, the Regent surmised that perhaps the real problem was that Tsangyang Gyatso kept bad company. Clearly, even a reincarnation of a great lama may be affected by the influences he encounters in this life too. One friend in particular was blamed for being a bad influence on the Dalai Lama. So, true to form, in the interests of the state, the Regent arranged to have him murdered. Unfortunately the target, together with his servant and Tsangyang Gyatso, had all exchanged clothes for fun while they were out for the night. Thus the servant was stabbed to death by mistake. When the assassins realized their error they set upon the right target, injuring him too. For his part, the

Dalai Lama immediately set about finding the assassins, using the State Oracle. He then had them executed. But no doubt he also suspected who had put them up to this murderous attack. From now on his relations with the Regent cooled still further.

We are reaching the end of our tragedy. In an atmosphere of growing unhappiness with the rule of the Sixth Dalai Lama in some influential international circles, in 1703 the Regent handed over power to his son. Nevertheless he retained control of the state from behind the scenes. Meanwhile a new Mongol Khan had come to power. Lha bzang (Lajang) Khan murdered his elder brother to become leader of the Khoshuud Mongol clan. From his great-grandfather, Gushri Khan, he also succeeded as the true 'king' of Tibet. And Lha bzang Khan wanted full influence and more power. The Regent (Sangyay Gyatso) did not agree. First he tried to poison Lha bzang Khan, but the plot was discovered. He tried another similar murderous scheme, but the monks from the great monasteries rejected it. Eventually, to cut a long and murky story short, Lha bzang Khan (perhaps understandably and with Chinese agreement) invaded central Tibet. The Tibetan defenders, fighting for the Regent, were completely defeated. The Regent was captured. It is not clear whether Lha bzang Khan himself was responsible, or one of his fierce Mongol wives who was also a general in command of the Mongol forces. Either way the Regent was beheaded. In spite of his skill in so many fields, it was all in the end too much for Desi Sangyay Gyatso. He had lost.

So, in the long run, had Tsangyang Gyatso and the Tibetans. Lha bzang Khan still had to do something with the Sixth Dalai Lama, who had been placed there by the Regent. However one looked at it, the Sixth Dalai Lama was a rival to Lha bzang Khan. So he had to go. Clearly – and perhaps genuinely for the Khan – this Dalai Lama could not be the real reincarnation of the Great Fifth. But Lha bzang Khan had already accepted the suzerainty of the K'ang-hsi Manchu Chinese emperor. Any attempt to depose the Dalai Lama would require the emperor's agreement. The agreement was not long in coming. The emperor needed a strong hand in Tibet, for there were other Mongol clans that could interfere otherwise, notably the powerful Dzungar Mongols who were opposed to China. The current Dalai Lama was useless. It was at this point that Lha bzang Khan put pressure on the abbots of the leading monasteries to declare Tsangyang Gyatso not the true Dalai Lama. Accordingly the abbots declared that his connection with Avalokiteśvara, whatever that was, had been broken. The Dalai Lama was deposed.

The Mongols led Tsangyang Gyatso away under arrest. The plan was apparently to take him to China or at least in the direction of China. But monks from Drepung monastery rescued him. When asked, the State Oracle gave a somewhat ambiguous reply but seemed to suggest that he was nevertheless the genuine reincarnation of the Fifth Dalai Lama. And that was the view of the overwhelming majority of Tibetans at that time and since. When the Mongols under Lha bzang Khan began to attack, Tsangyang Gyatso is said to have given himself up in order to prevent bloodshed. But perhaps there is some uncertainty about this too. It is reported that the Dalai Lama's companions, who walked towards the Mongol army with him, perished to the last man. Were they fighting? One wonders whether the Dalai Lama could have surrendered without even this bloodshed.

It is even less clear what happened next. According to Chinese and Mongol sources the Dalai Lama fell ill as he was being taken to China. He finally died in November 1706 in the far northeast near Kokonor Lake. It is said that at the time of his death he was reciting the mantra of Avalokiteśvara. His body may have been cremated, although the K'ang-hsi emperor, who accepted that he was not the genuine Dalai Lama, asked that the body simply be discarded. The Sixth Dalai Lama is the only Dalai Lama whose body is not preserved in Lhasa. Needless to say, there remains to the present day some suspicion that he may have been murdered. After all, he was no longer accepted as the true Dalai Lama by either Lha bzang Khan or the Chinese emperor. It would be best if he were out of the way.

In the meantime Lha bzang Khan had announced that a young monk that he had discovered was the true reincarnation of the Great Fifth Dalai Lama. This was not widely accepted. Twenty-two months after the reported death of Tsangyang Gyatso a child later recognized as the true Seventh Dalai Lama was born. But it seems that by now the Dalai Lamas had had enough of young women: the Seventh spent his life as a learned scholar and a monk.

Lha bzang Khan was eventually defeated in battle by the Dzungar Mongols and went down fighting bravely. It is said he took 11 Mongol soldiers with him. The Dzungars wreaked complete havoc on Lhasa and central Tibet, thereby losing what Tibetan support they had initially enjoyed as opponents of Lha bzang Khan. Eventually the Chinese, with Tibetan allies, stepped in to bring the Seventh Dalai Lama to Lhasa and (as far as the Chinese emperor was concerned) to establish some sort of firm control over Tibet. The rest, as they say, is history.

But not quite. There are also strange legends and rumours. Did Tsangyang Gyatso, the Sixth Dalai Lama, really die in 1706? There remains an account accepted even by some modern scholars (including apparently the current Tibetan refugee authorities in India) that has him escaping his Mongol escort. According to this account, well known among the Mongols, he lived anonymously, initially as a wandering pilgrim, for a further 40 years. He concealed his identity but was occasionally recognized. He visited China and India, and eventually died an abbot in the far northeast, on the Chinese border. There his body remains mummified.

This post-mortem life of the Sixth Dalai Lama is one of a wandering holy man. It bears little resemblance to his life prior to his 'death'. One might think that if Tsangyang Gyatso finally gained the freedom he so craved he would have done something other than become a pilgrim and eventually a dGe lugs pa abbot. It would also follow, of course, that at the time he was 'reincarnated' as the Seventh Dalai Lama, the Sixth Dalai Lama was still alive and well, living incognito. Nevertheless the historian Michael Aris, in his careful study, has argued that while it seems to stretch credibility to think that this story really applies to Tsangyang Gyatso, there is enough evidence to suggest something, or rather someone, behind it all. After all, the earliest account is found in a source that comes from a pupil of the man himself. This story, at least the part that refers to him in Mongolia and dying an abbot in the northeast, apparently is not mere fiction but refers to an actual person. And it seems that that person occasionally let it out to favoured pupils that really he was Tsangyang Gyatso, the Sixth Dalai Lama. The upshot of Aris's study is quite simply that there was an imposter. His real name, Aris shows, was Ngag dbang chos grags rgya mtsho (pronounced 'Ngawang Cherdrak Gyatso'). And he is presumably still there, mummified, in Tibet. Or Mongolia. Or China.

Or is it, after all, the body of the repentant Sixth Dalai Lama?

The sexy Dalai Lama?

The thing that often strikes Western readers coming to the story of the Sixth Dalai Lama for the first time is the fact – and there is no question that it is a fact – that he had sex with young women. This is a matter that seems to concern some people, and a matter that requires some sort of special explanation. It may also have concerned the Manchu Chinese emperor then, and it seems to interest Chinese Communist propagandists to the present day, concerned to blacken the institution of the Dalai Lamas and the Tibetan system whereby monks are involved in ruling the state.

But we need to be clear that in Tibet at the time it was unlikely that his sexual interests were what caused the scandal of the Sixth Dalai Lama. He was the Dalai Lama, considered an 'emanation' of Avalokiteśvara. And all agree that a great bodhisattva, in always acting for the benefit of others, might behave in a manner not expected by those of us who are less enlightened. As we have seen, there is a Tibetan tradition that the Great Fifth Dalai Lama had sex with women and even fathered a son – the Regent himself. Moreover it did not concern Tibetans, or indeed anyone else, when the government of the Fifth Dalai Lama, undoubtedly with his approval, executed criminals or political enemies. Killing is no less acceptable for a good Buddhist monk than is sex. Of course, a bodhisattva acting for the benefit of all sentient beings can kill with impunity. But then, he or she can also have sex. We know, for example, that in 1904, at the time of the Thirteenth Dalai Lama, the highest dGe lugs pa lama in Mongolia, the rJe btsun dam pa of Urga (pronounced 'Jetsun Dampa'), while supposedly a celibate monk was openly married. He also drank very heavily and smoked even in the presence of the Dalai Lama himself. This lama was ranked third in the dGe lugs religious hierarchy of the Tibetan state. While his behaviour was not approved by the 'Great Thirteenth', there is no evidence that it caused Mongolians and Tibetans to doubt the man, the incarnation or his Buddhism. The general view, apparently, was that he behaved in this way perhaps as a means of testing or strengthening the faith of his Buddhist followers.[68]

So doctrinally, as far as Tibetan Buddhism is concerned, and also socially among Tibetans, the sexual behaviour of Tsangyang Gyatso need not have been in itself a cause for undue concern. It is thus not necessary to defend, as do Norbu and Turnbull, or Hoffmann,[69] the sexuality of Tsangyang Gyatso by recourse to the possibility that he may really have been practising advanced tantric sexual techniques. In the case of Norbu and Turnbull one detects a certain concern to defend the Sixth Dalai Lama against the attacks of Chinese Communist propagandists. Norbu, as an abbot and the elder brother of the current Dalai Lama, had himself barely escaped from Chinese-occupied Tibet. There is also some hint that for Western readers Tantra might be a more acceptable explanation of the Dalai Lama's behaviour than simple sex. But that is our problem, not (traditionally) one for Tibetans.

Evidence that the Sixth Dalai Lama's affairs were related to the advanced tantric practice of sexual yoga is all but lacking from the verses themselves. A verse is sometimes cited: 'Never have I slept without a girl / Never have I lost a single drop of sperm.'[70] If this were true, and the verse genuinely by Tsangyang Gyatso, it would suggest a very advanced practice of sexual Tantra indeed (or impotence). An ability to reverse the flow of normal male orgasm and use the great bliss generated for psycho-physical sexual yoga is on all counts accepted by Tibetans as supremely advanced and (not surprisingly) difficult to master. But this verse consists of just two lines; it is in a nine-syllable metre rather than the six syllables of all the other verses and it is not included in any of the extant old Tibetan versions of the collected songs of Tsangyang Gyatso. There is clearly no reason to accept its authenticity. The only verse that does suggest directly the possibility of some form of tantric practice is verse 20. Interestingly this is not obviously related to Tsangyang Gyatso's relationships with women at all. Its only relevance here is in its suggestion of a tantric alchemical potion for avoiding hell. For a direct tantric explanation of Tsangyang Gyatso's sexual involvement this verse is of marginal significance (for further comments, see my notes on this verse).

We sometimes find a suggestion that the Dalai Lama's teachers, recognizing his interest in sex, would naturally have channelled it towards sexual yoga.[71] I find this unconvincing as an explanation for his behaviour:

1. The dGe lugs tradition has always favoured a strict control on the use of an actual consort (i.e. a real, live woman) in even advanced tantric practice. They were, after all, 'the Virtuous Ones'. They were founded on the basis of a strict adherence to monastic rule and other moral codes. The great Tsong kha pa himself, founder of the dGe lugs tradition, is said to have reached a stage where he could employ a physical consort, but declined to do so in order not to set a bad example to his followers. I doubt that even in the case of a Dalai Lama his teachers would encourage the use of a consort simply as a means of channelling sexual interest.

2. Moreover, if the Dalai Lama's teachers had chosen this option then they would probably have used as few young women as possible, and the sexual yoga would have been performed deep within the Potala Palace. Actually the exact opposite was the case. The Dalai Lama met his partners – it seems clear there were many – outside the Potala, either in his own rooms that he had built for the purpose overlooking one of the lakes, or in brothels, or sometimes elsewhere in Tibet.

3. As far as dGe lugs understanding of Tantra is concerned, the use of an actual consort for physical sex is a supremely advanced practice.[72] It is unlikely that the Dalai Lama's dGe lugs teachers would have encouraged him to use actual women at his age, particularly when his religious education had hardly begun. As far as the dGe lugs tradition was concerned he was nowhere near the level of learning and experience that would lead to much practical engagement with even relatively routine tantric practice.

4. In the last analysis we have to rely on the witness of the verses, having established to the best of our ability which verses are likely to be authentic. Those verses can give us as close an insight as we are ever likely to get into the actual mind of the Sixth Dalai Lama. Several verses (such as 1, 17, 18 and 19) suggest that Tsangyang Gyatso's attachment to his lover was such as to interfere with even basic Buddhist spiritual, particularly meditational, practice. In this he was, as we might perhaps expect, a beginner. The ability in concentration required for advanced tantric sexual yoga is phenomenal. Tsangyang Gyatso himself declares that when his lover is absent he cannot concentrate at all. If his concentration is that weak, it is doubtful that he could do much better at the time of orgasm.

5. There would have been no need to channel the Dalai Lama's interest in sex towards sexual yoga. I am suggesting that discreet sexual relations by the Dalai Lama would not as such have been a great problem for Tibetans, or in Lhasa. There was no real problem in his sex being straightforward, ordinary sex. Even before he handed back his monastic vows, the Dalai Lama was not a fully ordained monk. Technically he was a novice. He did not take the full monk's vows. Of course an ordinary novice would still be expected to avoid sexual contact with women, but the Dalai Lama was not an ordinary novice. And after not taking the full vows of a monk, and renouncing his novice's vows, the Dalai Lama was a layman and as entitled to have sex with women as any other layman, including the Regent. There is even a verse to this effect:

Do not tell me
"Tsangyang! You are dissolute,"
Just as you desire pleasure
I, too, desire pleasure and comfort.[73]

This verse is not included in the official collections of his poems, and is undoubtedly not by Tsangyang Gyatso. But no matter. It shows how the Tibetan people considered his sexual activity. Put frankly, as a layman Tsangyang Gyatso was just having fun. It would have been considered unnecessary to introduce him to the complexities of advanced tantric sexual techniques, particularly when it is

doubtful that dGe lugs teachers themselves had more than a theo-
retical understanding of their practice.

There is simply no substantial evidence from the verses of any
interest in sexual yoga. I suggest that it never crossed the Dalai
Lama's mind to bother with the discipline of advanced tantric sexual
yoga. That was not what he wanted. To read the verses this way is
to impose upon them a model which is unnecessary and which loses
the simple pungency, the passion and the sadness of the verses
themselves. Moreover, in spite of a modern claim encountered
sometimes that Tibetans incline to read the Sixth Dalai Lama's
verses as indicating advanced tantric practice,[74] even if true, I doubt
that this strategy is a traditional one. I strongly suspect that this way
of reading the verses reflects precisely the changed (modern, West-
ern) world of the Tibetan diaspora since the Chinese occupation in
the 1950s. If not a more puritanical world, this is at least a world that
has different expectations of religious practitioners. In support of my
contention here, we could cite Sir Charles Bell's experience (noted
above) in Tibet prior to the Chinese takeover that the behaviour of
the rJe btsun dam pa of Urga was explained not as advanced tantric
yoga but rather as testing the faith of his devotees. Similarly, later in
the twentieth century, during the minority of the present Fourteenth
Dalai Lama, the Regent, Reting (*Rwa sgreng*) Rinpoche, a monk,
was known to have a penchant for both men and women.[75] Yet it was
not that which in itself led to his downfall or indeed caused him
particular problems.

Moreover both the Thirteenth and the Fourteenth Dalai Lamas
have commented on the behaviour of the Sixth Dalai Lama. Both, of
course, are Tibetan Buddhists and consider him to have been the
genuine reincarnation of the powerful Great Fifth Dalai Lama.
Therefore both consider the Sixth to have had at some level the
powers and the abilities of the Fifth, as well as being an 'emanation'
of Avalokiteśvara. Thus both the Thirteenth and the Fourteenth
accept the spiritual distinction of the Sixth Dalai Lama, without
recourse to a tantric explanation for his behaviour. Both, on the
other hand, consider the Sixth to have behaved (for some reason)

improperly and disastrously in the public sphere. Thus the Thirteenth Dalai Lama commented:

> He did not observe even the rules of a fully ordained priest. He drank wine habitually. And he used to have his body in several places at the same time, e.g. in Lhasa, in Kong-po (a province seven days' journey east of Lhasa), and elsewhere. Even the place where he retired to the Honourable Field (i.e. died) is uncertain; one tomb of his [i.e. Aris's impostor] is in Alashar in Mongolia, while there is another in the Rice Heap [Drepung] monastery. Showing many bodies at the same time is disallowed in all the sects of our religion, because it causes confusion in the work. One of his bodies used to appear in the crowd in the Reception Hall of the seventh Dalai Lama. One is said to appear also at my receptions, but I am unable to say whether this is true or not.[76]

In support of the suggestion that many bodies might be the answer, a Tibetan friend of Sir Charles Bell commented that '[t]he Sixth Dalai Lama had the power of assuming several forms. His own body used to be in the Potala Palace, while a secondary body used to roam about, drink wine, and keep women.'[77] It seems that a Dalai Lama can have his cake and eat it.

And the Fourteenth on the Sixth Dalai Lama:

> [H]e was spiritually pre-eminent, but politically, he was weak and disinterested. He could not follow the Vth Dalai Lama's path. This was a great failure.[78]

This, I suggest, is as close as they can come to condemning what we unenlightened beings see of the behaviour of Tsangyang Gyatso – his refusal to adopt the traditional role of a Dalai Lama. This must include the expected public vows of celibacy and sexual discretion. It is noticeable that neither the Thirteenth nor the Fourteenth (nor Bell's informant) considers that a tantric explanation will suffice for the behaviour of the Sixth. We could also mention the verse cited above that does (I suggest) indicate how Tibetans really saw the sexual behaviour of the Sixth Dalai Lama. He was entitled to have pleasure and fun. The problem was how he chose to do it.

Moreover, while we find material that explains the many re-markable abilities of the Sixth Dalai Lama, abilities that all Tibetans would expect of a genuine Dalai Lama, we do not find advanced sexual yoga used in pre-modern sources as an explanation for the Sixth Dalai Lama's involvement with women. Tsepon W.D. Shakabpa, writing his history of Tibet soon after the modern Chinese occupation, based mainly on traditional Tibetan sources, and himself a traditional Tibetan of the 'older generation', makes no attempt whatsoever to explain or justify Tsangyang Gyatso's liking for young women. The Dalai Lama's renouncing of his monastic vows is explained by the fact that he 'was of a different turn of mind'. The vows 'did not appeal to him'.[79] It is striking that Shakabpa makes no mention whatsoever of any tantric involvement of the Sixth Dalai Lama that might explain his sexual interests. One can be reasonably sure therefore that the traditional Tibetan sources available to him also made no mention of it.[80] And this is not surprising. To the extent that Tibetans consider the Dalai Lama as Avalokiteśvara incarnate, and thus possessed of wonderful powers and abilities, they consider him already a Buddha and beyond the need for yoga (or conventional morality) of any kind, including sexual yoga. The highest tantric practices aim at enlightenment in one lifetime, but the Dalai Lama is considered by ordinary Tibetans already enlightened (but see his own verse 19).

Indeed, the precognizant powers of a Dalai Lama are employed in one other pre-modern explanation for his behaviour that circulated among some Tibetans. It is that he was actually trying to father a child in order to found a dynasty. He knew in advance that if he could do so his dynasty would become powerful and change in some way the future of Tibet.[81] If this were true, then clearly Tsangyang Gyatso's ability to tell the future was limited, since as far as we know he did not succeed in having a son. The explanation of Sir Charles Bell's Tibetan friend for this failure is that had he succeeded, a powerful dynasty would have led inevitably to violence, and the Buddhist religion in Tibet would have declined. Thus it did not happen. But actually the only verse of the Dalai Lama related to the possibility of children (verse 28) rather suggests an attempt to shirk responsibility for their upbringing. At least, Tsangyang Gyatso does not envisage the upbringing of a prince.[82]

Moreover, I doubt very much that an explanation in terms of procreation will suffice for Tsangyang Gyatso's sexual interests. For all the problems of rule by reincarnation, the Dalai Lama as a hereditary institution would not have been an obvious solution to the problems of Tibetan government at that time. Tibet had had kings in the past, indeed in the not-too-distant past. Tibet already had a secular ruler – the Mongol Khan. Any attempt to found a hereditary dynasty would fall foul of the great monasteries, the Mongol Khan and the powerful Manchu Chinese emperor. And by definition, any child of Tsangyang Gyatso would not be the Dalai Lama, since he could not be the *reincarnation* of the Sixth Dalai Lama. There would thus be no basis for any claim to a significant relationship with Avalokiteśvara – at least, not a significant relationship based on the activities of previous Dalai Lamas. As we have seen, there was a view circulating in some circles that the Regent, Desi Sangyay Gyatso, was the illegitimate son of the Fifth Dalai Lama. But there was no suggestion that this might replace the reincarnating Dalai Lamas with a hereditary dynasty. One could not imagine ordinary Tibetans finding 'Son of Dalai' a satisfactory alternative to 'Dalai Himself' (as a reincarnation).

Anyway, one thing is clear. While some Tibetans felt there must be some sort of explanation for the sexual interests of the Sixth Dalai Lama other than his age and sex, prior to modern times there does not seem to have been recourse to an explanation in terms of tantric sexual yoga.

So I am suggesting that, contrary to what we might think, the Sixth Dalai Lama's sexual behaviour would not in itself have caused great problems in pre-modern Tibet.[83] This was not what generated the real scandal. But then what *did* cause the scandal? For scandal there was, a scandal that led eventually to the deaths of the Regent and the Dalai Lama, and extended Chinese (Manchu) control in Tibet. This control has also provided in recent times, alas, an effective basis for justifying the twentieth-century Chinese takeover of Tibet, as forming 'an integral part of the motherland'.

It seems to me that what really caused the scandal was the Dalai Lama's refusal to be discreet and his complete lack of interest in playing the game. He refused to take the full vows of a monk. He returned to the lay state, and he dressed flamboyantly as a layman. He would rather go off with his friends and attendants to archery competitions. The Dalai Lama also built – or had built – an exquisite 'stately pleasure dome' in the gardens of the Potala, testifying to his aesthetic taste. He roamed the streets and brothels, drank alcohol publicly and enjoyed pranks with his friends. One prank, as we have seen, even saved the life of a friend.

Tsangyang Gyatso had little interest in his role as the Dalai Lama. He had no interest whatsoever in the murky world of contemporary Tibetan politics. We need to remember that it was only nine years between the official declaration of his 'discovery', with his release from virtual house arrest, and his (apparent) death. The scandal that occurred was not in his personal tastes but in his public persona. It was his refusal to adopt his public role at a very sensitive time in Tibetan history. We sometimes find modern books that aim to portray the Sixth Dalai Lama as 'The Rebel' – a 1960s-type revolutionary against puritanical sexual restrictions and control by the older generation of priestly power freaks. But in fact Tsangyang Gyatso, while refusing to accept the role imposed on him, rebelled only in insisting on having his own way regardless of the consequences. We find several verses in which the Dalai Lama shows he is at the time torn between a life of religion and his love affairs. But he fails to offer, either in his verses or in his behaviour, a critique of a particular brand of religion or indeed a particular political system except inasmuch as it restricts his own behaviour. Rather he seems to accept the orthodox dGe lugs pa state and religion. That is what gives him his dilemma. That is what makes his case so sad. In the end, verse 65 suggests, he simply decides to follow his heart in spite of what may happen.

It is this, I think, that also prompted the abbots to acquiesce (even if under pressure) in the claim that Avalokiteśvara's blessing, a blessing based on the Dalai Lama's immense vows of compassion in previous lives, had left Tsangyang Gyatso. For it seemed that the young Dalai Lama was not content to take a backstage role (even if he could) and leave public appearances to the Regent. Nor was he content to rule his people himself (or have it thought by the populace that he was doing so) as an orthodox dGe lugs pa monk Dalai Lama. In fact Tsangyang Gyatso seemed in the end (even after a certain amount of inner searching) to be interested in only his own pleasures. He was to all appearances completely lacking in concern for the wider world of Tibet and its neighbours. He was thus, at least to Tibetans directly involved in the murky politics of the time, apparently lacking in compassion. He was lacking in the very essence of what he should be as an emanation (or whatever) of Avalokiteśvara. And it was those, politically involved, Tibetans, Mongols and Chinese – not the ordinary politically naive Tibetans – who took the lead in trying to remove the Dalai Lama.

Tsangyang Gyatso found himself thrust into a role and a world he simply did not want. His response, his behaviour, was in many ways that of a typical adolescent, an adolescent now come into unexpected wealth after years of rather horrible deprivation. In saying this, I am not intending to disparage him in any way. He behaved as I suspect most of us would have done under the circumstances, at least at that age. He had so little say in his own future. He was perhaps aware of what could happen to him and to Tibet, but he probably did not think until the end that it would. At least, not to him. In not really expecting the worst to happen Tsangyang Gyatso was yet again like a modern adolescent. No normal healthy teenager really thinks they will ever die. Hence his complaint in verse 58 that it had all been so unfair. In that we can just hear the voice of the 24-year-old, dying long before his time and having been effectively imprisoned for half of those years. Tsangyang Gyatso's life was in the end not much fun. And we should not forget it.

He was right – it was all so unfair. Therein lies his tragedy, and that is what makes his songs so sad as well as often rather beautiful. Those who would turn Tsangyang Gyatso into a hippie rebel, 'the Outsider', or a tantric holy man or a frustrated benevolent ruler of his people destroy (I suggest) the sadness of his story and the beauty of his verses. Tsangyang Gyatso spent his time trying to tell everyone that he was simply a normal ordinary human being who wanted to live the life of a normal human being. If he couldn't get through to them by his words, he could try and do it with his actions. But one way or another they wanted to make him be more. They would destroy the person he was. And that is what they still try to do, those who would make him some kind of icon to more than just his own personal tragedy.

How to read the verses of the Sixth Dalai Lama

I have argued that in most cases the attempt to read the verses of the Sixth Dalai Lama as statements of obscure Tibetan religion or tantric sexual yoga, beyond their apparent surface meaning, seems to me to be far-fetched. There are also some that would mine the verses for hidden references to the Dalai Lama's political position. This approach appears to be particularly favoured by modern Chinese writers, perhaps reflecting the Communist regime's interest in politics and the economic determinants of power. I also find this in most cases unconvincing. Sorensen too seems to give the 'hidden political reference' much more credence than I would. Thus, just to take one verse at random (44):

tshes gsum zla ba dkar ba
dkar gos nang nas chod song
bco lnga'i nam dang mnyam pa'i
zhal bzhes cig kyang gnang zhu

The three-day moon is bright,
Completely clothed in white.
Please, will you promise me
Time just like the full-moon?

Here, Sorensen observes,

[W]e may ... see the moon's phases as an illustration of the stages in the God-king's attempt to appropriate power. Evidently, the young ruler could perhaps temporarily settle for a modest share of power, but his urgent quest for real rulership, prompted him to request for the 'full' access or the 'full' display of power.[84]

The assumption here is that Tsangyang Gyatso was indeed very interested in his political role. He was blocked from fulfilling it by figures like the Regent and Lha bzang Khan. The evidence for this approach to the Sixth Dalai Lama appears to lie in just such a 'deep' reading of the verses. I find this logic weak. It seems to presuppose what it sets out to show. I also find such readings, while sometimes vaguely interesting, largely unconvincing. So I shall not consider them further.

Still, my translation in the main leaves it quite open for the reader if he or she wishes to choose to give the verses some religious or political interpretation other than – or as well as – what appears to be the straightforward erotic meaning. There are some that find the Dalai Lama's interest in young women, or his apparent political ineptitude, embarrassing. They are perfectly free, as far as possible within the limits of this translation, to superimpose upon the surface level of the text an additional, symbolic reading. I do not do so myself. To me these verses say and mean what they say. That is all. They are mostly about the Sixth Dalai Lama's loves and his frustrations. To that extent the best way to read these verses is in the light of Tsangyang Gyatso's own personal story, as (in the main) very tragic love poems.

Until recently there has been no critical edition of the Sixth Dalai Lama's verses. There is one now, produced with a great deal of hard work by Per Sorensen (1990) and drawing on a wide acquaintance with the Indo-Tibetan tradition of written and oral poetry and folksongs. Unfortunately this edition has been ignored by, for example, the Fields and Cutillo translation of 1998 (*The Turquoise Bee*). As a result Fields and Cutillo comment that there is as yet no definitive edition of the Songs (p 27). They therefore include every verse they are acquainted with and attributed to Tsangyang Gyatso as being by him, including the verse quoted above on sperm. Inclusion of this verse in particular as being by Tsangyang Gyatso can give a very decided tantric slant on how we interpret the Dalai Lama's affairs. Sorensen himself, on the other hand, expresses considerable caution as to whether any of the verses attributed to him are actually by Tsangyang Gyatso.[85] It seems to me that this caution should be borne in mind. The verses certainly reflect in metric and verse structure, and frequently in flavour, a popular Tibetan tradition of anonymous political song. Until the takeover of Tibet by China in

the 1950s such political songs often served as a means by which
public opinion could be gauged and disagreement with the state
voiced.[86] It is indeed quite possible that a number of the songs
attributed to Tsangyang Gyatso originated this way. That is, they
express popular and anonymous songs that circulated in Lhasa as a
criticism of the Dalai Lama or the Regent, and indicate not so much
the Dalai Lama's own sentiments as those of others, showing how he
and his acquaintances were seen. Verse 54 in particular could be an
example. Verse 39, if it is taken as being about Tsangyang Gyatso
himself and not the Dalai Lama referring to the Regent, may be
another. And the famous verse about his reincarnation in Lithang
(verse 57) probably originated long after the event. Aris mentions
that he has not found this verse mentioned anywhere in the Tibetan
literature of the eighteenth and nineteenth centuries.[87] The first
blockprinted edition of the songs dates from perhaps the late
eighteenth century.

Nevertheless, while an anonymous folk origin of any of these
verses is always a decided possibility, I incline to a conservative
approach here. Sorensen's edition includes 66 verses. Within this
edition I accept a verse as probably by Tsangyang Gyatso unless I
have particular reason to doubt its authenticity. In particular some of
the verses, it seems to me, are sufficiently personal to stem from the
Dalai Lama himself. Examples would be verses like 31–3, that refer to
illness brought on by his situation. He ought to know about his own
illnesses. Scepticism can go only so far.

So how are we to read these verses? I suggest, with pleasure in
whatever way (knowing the historical story) you gain your pleasure.
For that reason it has been of particular importance to me to
translate the verses combining appropriate accuracy with something
that also works well in English verse. The *Notes for Appreciation*
contains additional information that I think might enhance the
pleasure and understanding of these verses.

The present translation

Like common Tibetan folk and political songs, these verses consist
mainly of four lines each. Three (verses 20, 50 and 56) are of six lines
each.[88] Tibetan is (or it is now) a monosyllabic language. This means

that each syllable has a separate meaning or use within the language. Many expressions are made of two syllables, a main one and a modifier, often *pa*, or *ba*, or *ma*, or *po*, or *bo*, or *mo*. Thus, for example, we might find *dag pa* (purity). The effect of this on Tibetan sound patterns is in terms of a stressed sound followed by an unstressed one (˘˘). This is known in the study of metres as a trochaic foot (contrasted with an iambic foot (˘˘)). Thus the nature of the Tibetan language enables it naturally to fall into lines of trochaic metre. The Sixth Dalai Lama's verses each consist of six syllables to a line, alternating heavy and light stress. Each line is thus three trochaic feet. The metre can be known therefore as a 'trochaic trimetre':

‾˘ ‾˘ ‾˘
‾˘ ‾˘ ‾˘
‾˘ ‾˘ ‾˘
‾˘ ‾˘ ‾˘

Let us take as an example the famous verse 54:

po ta la ru bzhugs dus
rig 'dzin tshangs dbyangs rgya mtsho
lha sa zhol du sdod dus
'chal po dwangs bzang dbang po

In Potala dwelling –
Rigdzin Tsangyang Gyatso.
Lhasa and Zhol roaming –
Screwer Dangzang Wangbo!

Tibetan, as you can see, looks unpronounceable. That rather obscures the metre for one who does not know Tibetan. This is because the spelling now bears little relationship to the way it is pronounced in Lhasa. An approximate version for our purposes here of the pronunciation for an English speaker would be:

po ta la ru zhuk du
rik dzin tsang yang gya tso
hla sa zhol du derr du
chel bo dang zang wong bo

It is now possible to see the six syllable format of these verses. If you were to sing them, you would no doubt appreciate even more the heavy–light stress structure.[89] The Tibetan does not have to use rhyme (although we do have alternate rhyming ends in this particular verse). It does use alliteration and puns. It is also able to make points through the use of, or the failure to use, honorifics. In Tibetan it is common to use different words when the speaker refers to someone considered superior. This can be employed to poetic effect. It is very uncommon to use an honorific for oneself. But in the verse above the author uses an honorific verb translated as 'dwelling', and a non-honorific actually with the same meaning but here translated for effect in English as 'roaming'. It seems to me that the result is to emphasize the respect given by people to the Dalai Lama in the Potala, and the common coarseness of the 'Screwer' – actually the same (almost) Jekyll-and-Hyde character.

Central to this type of Tibetan verse, however, is its rhythm. For this reason, although the Tibetan of many of Tsangyang Gyatso's verses is extremely compressed, nevertheless, in spite of the difficulty, it seems to me that the six-syllable structure of the original is worth trying to preserve in order to keep something like that distinctive rhythm. It brings to the fore the complex simplicity of these verses, as well as their metric uniformity. Of course English does not naturally fall into a trochaic metre, and iambic suits English much better. But I have translated as far as possible preserving the six-syllable line, sometimes at the cost of strict literalness, and I have also used English alliteration and some English puns. English is a particularly good medium for alliterative verse – it is central to the very earliest English verse such as *Beowulf.* I have not tried to match the Tibetan alliteration. But I have tried to use the resources of the English language that, combined with the Tibetan metrical structure, can make something pleasant to read in English. I appear to have been the first to venture to publish a complete translation of these verses keeping to the Tibetan six-syllable pattern. Bell rather hints that it might be impossible.[90] I may be foolish. But it has been fun to do, and (I think) it is more fun to read.

To illustrate further some features and difficulties of my transla-
tion when compared with others, perhaps we can look at just one
more verse (45):

sa bcu'i dbyings su bzhugs pa'i
sa chui ying su zhuk pay
stage ten-of sphere-on dwelling [honorific]-of

dam can rdo rje chos skyong
dam chen dor jay cherr kyong
pledge-bearing Dorje dharma protector

mthu dang nus pa yod na
tu dang nerr ba yerr na
power and ability exists if/when

bstan pa'i dgra bo sgrol dang
ten pay dra wo drol dang
teaching-of enemy liberate [imperative]

O Dharma Protector,
Ten-stage-dwelling, pledge-bound,
Dorje – if strong, able –
Please free the Teaching's foes.

The second line of the Tibetan is the pronunciation. The third line
is, as far as possible, a literal word-by-word translation. You can see
that my translation here, as it stands, is also reasonably literal given
English syntactical requirements. It keeps to the six-syllable metre.

Nevertheless this is a particularly difficult verse to translate within
the six-syllable format. The verse has nothing to do with love, and
quite possibly does not come from the Sixth Dalai Lama. It is an
invocation to one of the Protectors of the Buddha's teaching
(Dharma). These are wrathful in appearance, bound by pledge to
uphold and protect Buddhism and its practitioners, and they are also
the beings that commonly possess the Tibetan oracle-mediums. The
Tibetan *dam can* here could mean 'superior', or 'holy', (= *dam pa* +
can) as with some of the other translations. But in context I suspect
it means 'pledge-bound', as in *dam bca' can*. At least it has also this
implication. This also makes for a better English verse. The protec-

tor here is just called 'Dorje' (*rDo rje*) – in Sanskrit, the *Vajra* – the 'Diamond' or 'Thunderbolt', a common name associated with Tantric Buddhism. In context it could well be rDo rje grags ldan (pronounced 'Dorje Drakden'), the Dalai Lama's own protector. If this verse is by the Sixth Dalai Lama, perhaps he wrote it when consulting the oracle in order to find out who the murderers were who killed his friend's servant. Any foes of the Dalai Lama would certainly be thought of as foes of Buddhism. The Protector is described as dwelling in (the realm of) the ten stages. These are the ten stages of the career of a bodhisattva. It may mean that 'Dorje' himself is a bodhisattva, or that he protects those on the bodhisattva path. If one takes the Tibetan as referring to the tenth stage, rather than ten stages, then it is possible to take this verse as suggesting that the Protector resides in the final stage of the bodhisattva's career, almost himself a Buddha. 'Strong' translates *mthu*, which really includes magical power as well. In verse 37, for poetic reasons in context, I have translated it as 'charms'. The reference to 'freeing' (or liberating) in the last line (Tibetan *sgrol*) is literal, but it is an expression commonly used in certain Tibetan tantric literature for killing. Sorensen prefers a meaning of 'expelling', driving off. But Tsangyang Gyatso certainly had executed those responsible for the attack on him, his friend and the servant. In this very tantric context I do not see any grounds for thinking that it has any other meaning than 'kill'. In particular I do not think any sense of 'liberate', i.e. enlightenment, can possibly be meant here. That is not what Dharma-protectors do.

For interest my translation can be compared with the following translations, each from relatively recent complete translations of the Sixth Dalai Lama's verses. Only that by Sorensen uses or even takes into consideration his critical edition and its extensive commentary. Constant reference to Sorensen, it seems to me, is now necessary for any attempt at translating these verses, and Sorensen's critical edition is the one I have used for my translation and for the Tibetan original. Once or twice I have differed from Sorensen in the Tibetan text I have used. These divergences are mentioned in my *Notes for Appreciation*. Sorensen's translations, on the other hand, while literal are rather unpoetic and sometimes show evidence that he is not a native English speaker.

The translations here are in chronological order. The editions by Dhondup, Barks, and Fields and Cutillo are listed (on the Amazon website) as still available. The Houston translation has been completely superseded. The Barks 'translation' appears in fact to be a composite re-rendering of the translations of others, relying (as here, with a mispronunciation of the Tibetan *skyong* (kyong)) mainly on the Dhondup translation. It has no comment on the Tibetan text or on the meaning of the verses. It has not used Sorensen's critical edition, and taken as a whole is not at all reliable as a translation of the Sixth Dalai Lama's verses. I do not know whether the other translations are still available or not.

> Holy vajra, dharma-protector,
> Who abides in the tenth-stage realm;
> If you have the strength and power,
> Save the enemies of the teaching.
>
> (Tatz[91])

> The transcendent *Dorje Choskyong*
> The oracle of the Tenth Spiritual Stage
> If you have supernatural powers
> Destroy the foes of the *dharma*.
>
> (Dhondup[92])

> One with magical power
> As Dam Chen Dorjay
> In the perfect sphere,
> May destroy Dharma foes.
>
> (Houston[93])

> Holy [Medium] rDo-rje [Grags-ldan], Protector of the Law,
> Who resides over the sphere of the ten stages,
> If you possess magical power and potency
> Pray, ward off the foes of the Buddhist teaching!
>
> (Sorensen[94])

> Oracle of the Tenth Stage,
> Dorje Choskyang, if you have power,

Destroy those who hate the natural law.

(Barks[95])

Holy oracle Lama Dorje
Who abides in the state
just before Buddhahood –
If you have the power and ability
Liberate even the enemies of Dharma.

(Fields and Cutillo[96])

I do not want to comment further on these translations. Comparisons, as they say, are odious. Clearly, while some of these seem to me grammatically, semantically and poetically rather better than others, there is room for differences of translation and interpretation. Proper critical study of a translation, for those who do not know the original language, should always employ more than one translated version. On this particular verse most of the translations do not differ radically. That is by no means always the case. Partly, how much liberty one has in translating verse depends on how much space there is for explanation in notes. Sorensen alone gives a proper detailed commentary. In fixing the meaning of the verses within a Tibetan cultural context Sorensen's notes are indispensable. I do not think it would be possible to translate throughout the verses using a six-syllable format without fairly extensive annotations. But then, Tibetans too would need to rely either on their prior knowledge or on a commentary. It is obvious that we cannot expect to appropriate such literature without some sort of explanation. Nevertheless I think this verse shows that it is possible to translate (with notes) reasonably accurately and also in the same rhythm, and with the same complex simplicity, as the Tibetan.

ও ও ও ও ও ও ও

Songs of Love,
Poems of Sadness

ও ও ও ও ও ও ও

1

shar phyogs ri bo'i rtse nas
dkar gsal zla ba shar byung
ma skyes a ma'i zhal ras
yid la 'khor 'khor byas byung

ཆ ཆ ཆ ཆ ཆ

Above eastern mountains
Shone forth the moon, bright white.
Unbornmother – her face,
Circled before my mind.

2

na ning btab pa'i ljang gzhon
da lo sog ma'i phon lcog
pho gzhon rgas pa'i lus po
rwa co'i gzhu las gyong ba

ཚ ཚ ཚ ཚ ཚ

Green shoots planted last year
Today are stacked as straw.
Young man's body, growing,
Firmer than a horn bow.

3

rang sems song ba'i mi de
gtan gyi mdun mar byung na
rgya mtsho'i gting nas nor bu
lon pa de dang mnyam byung

ཚ ཚ ཚ ཚ ཚ

If she who stole my heart
Were to become my wife;
Like landing a jewel
Drawn from the ocean's depths.

4

'gro zhor lam bu'i snying thub
lus dri zhim pa'i bu mo
g.yu chung gru dkar brnyed nas
skyur ba de dang 'dra byung

ཚ་ ཚ་ ཚ་ ཚ་ ཚ་

A love met in passing,
Girl with the fragrant limbs;
Like finding rare turquoise –
And throwing it away.

5

mi chen dpon po'i sras mo
khams 'bras mtshar la bltas na
kham sdong mthon po'i rtse nas
'bras bu smin pa 'dra byung

ཆ ཆ ཆ ཆ ཆ

Lady, a Lord's daughter –
When I saw such a peach,
She was like a ripe fruit,
In the topmost branches.

6

sems pa phar la shor nas
mtshan mo'i gnyid thebs gcog gi
nyin mo lag tu ma lon
yid thang chad rogs yin pa

ཆ ཆ ཆ ཆ ཆ

So out of mind with love,
I lose my sleep at night.
Can't touch her while it's day —
Frustration's my sole friend.

7

me tog nam zla yal song
g.yu sbrang sems pa ma skyo
byams pa'i las 'phro zad par
nga ni skyo rgyu mi 'dug

ཆ ཆ ཆ ཆ ཆ

Flowering's time has fled –
The turquoise bee grieves not.
Finished fortune of love –
I too shall not lament.

8

rtsi thog ba mo'i kha la
skya ser rlung gi pho nya
me tog sbrang bu gnyis kyi
'bral mtshams byed mkhan los yin

ছ ছ ছ ছ ছ

Hoarfrost sugars the grass;
Messenger of the grey
yellow storm that truly
Parts the bloom from her bee.

9

ngang pa 'dam la chags nas
re zhig sdod dgos bsams kyang
mtsho mo dar kha 'grigs nas
rang sems kho thag chod song

ཪྠ ཪྠ ཪྠ ཪྠ ཪྠ

Wild goose, pining for fens,
Hoped to remain awhile.
On the lake mere ice sheets.
Hope too flew far away.

10

gru shan sems pa med kyang
rta mgos phyi mig bltas byung
khrel gzhung med pa'i byams pas
nga la phyi mig mi lta

ཋ ཋ ཋ ཋ ཋ

The ferry lacks feeling;
But its horse-head looked back.
My lover – so brazen –
Throws me never a glance.

11

nga dang tshong 'dus bu mo'i
tshig gsum dam bca'i mdud pa
khra bo'i sbrul la ma brgyab
rang rang sa la grol song

ཆ ཆ ཆ ཆ ཆ

With me, the market girl
Twined three words in a pledge.
Alone they soon unwind.
Might as well knot a snake!

12

chung 'dris byams pa'i rlung bskyed
lcang ma'i logs la btsugs yod
lcang srung a jo zhal ngos
rdo ka rgyag pa ma gnang

ཆ ཆ ཆ ཆ ཆ

For my love from childhood,
Prayer flags on a willow.
Guardian of Willows,
Sir, please do not throw stones!

13

bris pa'i yi ge nag chung
chu dang thig pas 'jig song
ma bris sems kyi ri mo
bsubs kyang zub rgyu mi 'dug

ཚ ཚ ཚ ཚ ཚ

Small black letters, written,
Vanish with water drops.
Mind pictures, unwritten,
Though effaced, will not fade.

14

brgyab pa'i nag chung the 'us
gsung skad 'byon ni mi shes
khrel dang gzhung gi the 'u
so so'i sems la skyon dang

ཆ ཆ ཆ ཆ ཆ

The small black seal, when stamped,
Still, knows not how to speak.
Rather, should we impress
Concern's seal on our hearts.

15

stong ldan ha lo'i me tog
mchod pa'i rdzas la phebs na
g.yu sbrang gzhon nu nga yang
lha khang nang la khrid dang

ཆ ཆ ཆ ཆ ཆ

Gorgeous hollyhock blooms,
If given in worship,
I, too – young turquoise bee –
Take me to the temple!

16

sems song bu mo mi bzhugs
dam pa'i chos la phebs na
pho gzhon nga yang mi sdod
ri khrod 'grim la thal 'gro

ཚ ཚ ཚ ཚ ཚ

If my sweetheart won't stay –
She's embraced religion –
I, too, am not staying.
I'm straight off on retreat!

17

mtshan ldan bla ma'i drung du
sems 'khrid zhu bar phyin pas
sems pa 'gor kyang mi thub
byams pa'i phyogs la shor song

ཐ ཐ ཐ ཐ ཐ

Before a great lama,
I asked for holy help.
No good – though thoughts delayed,
They slipped back to my love.

18

sgom pa'i bla ma zhal ras
yid la 'char rgyu mi 'dug
ma sgom byams pa'i zhal ras
yid la va le va le

ཆ་ ཆ་ ཆ་ ཆ་ ཆ་

Meditating – in mind,
No lama's face appears.
Unbidden, lover's face
In mind, so clearly clear.

19

sems pa 'di la 'gro 'gro
dam pa'i chos la phyin na
tshe gcig lus gcig nyid la
sangs rgyas thob pa'i 'dug go

ଛ ଛ ଛ ଛ ଛ

With thoughts on religion
That were ever for her,
One lifetime, one body –
I become a Buddha!

20

dag pa shel ri gangs chu
klu bdud rdo rje'i zil pa
bdud rtsi sman gyi phab rgyun
chang ma ye shes mkha' 'gro
dam tshig gtsang mas btung na
ngan song myong dgos mi 'dug

ཆ ཆ ཆ ཆ ཆ

Dakpashelri water,
Luderdorje dewdrops,
Yeast that is elixir,
Wisdom-ḍākinī serves.
Drunk with pure commitments –
You need not taste of hell.

21

rlung rta yar 'gro'i dus la
rlung bskyed dar lcog btsugs pas
mdzangs ma ma bzang bu mo'i
mgron po la ni bos byung

ཪ ཪ ཪ ཪ ཪ

At a time of good luck,
With my prayer flags flapping,
I was invited home
By a charming bright girl.

22

so dkar lpags pa'i 'dzum mdangs
bzhugs gral spyi la bltas na
mig zur khra mo'i sgril mtshams
gzhon pa'i gdong la bltas byung

ཚ ཚ ཚ ཚ ཚ

Taking in the whole row –
Laughing smiles, with white teeth.
Sidelong glance from bright eyes,
Thrown at my youthful face.

23

ha cang sems la song nas
'grogs 'dris e yong dris pas
'chi bral byed na min na
gson bral mi byed gsungs byung

ཆ ཆ ཆ ཆ ཆ

We're so madly in love.
'Together – forever?'
'Until death do us part',
She whispered, 'I'll be there'.

24

mdzangs ma'i thugs dang bstun na
tshe 'di'i chos skal chad 'gro
dben pa'i ri khrod 'grims na
bu mo'i thugs dang 'gal 'gro

ཆ ཆ ཆ ཆ ཆ

Suiting my bright one's heart,
I lose life's religion.
Heading forth, a hermit,
I belie my girl's heart.

25

sbrang bu rgya la bcug 'dra
kong phrug gzhon pa'i blo sna
zhag gsum nyal rogs byas pas
phugs yul lha chos dran byung

ཐ ཐ ཐ ཐ ཐ

He'd bedded her three days.
Like a bee in a web,
The Gongbo youth's fancies
Remembered religion.

26

gtan grogs khyod la bsams pa'i
khrel dang ngo tsha med na
mgo la rgyab pa'i gtsug gyus
skad cha smras ni mi shes

ཕ ཕ ཕ ཕ ཕ

Eternal friend, if you
Are shameless in your thoughts,
The turquoise on your head,
Would not know how to tell.

27

'dzum dang so dkar ston phyogs
gzhon pa'i blo khrid yin 'dug
snying nas sha tsha yod med
dbu mna' bzhes rogs gnang dang

ཆ ཆ ཆ ཆ ཆ

You smile, pretty white teeth –
Leading on the youth's mind.
Swear to me, please: Do I
Truly tempt you or not?

28

snying thub bya rdo lam 'phrad
a ma chang mas sbyar byung
lan chags bu lon byung na
'tsho skyong khyod ras gnang zhu

ཆ ཆ ཆ ཆ ཆ

As a bird meets a stone,
The madam joined lovers.
If there should be issue,
Please madam, will you pay!

29

snying gtam pha mar ma bshad
chung 'dris byams par bshad pas
byams pa shwa pho mang nas
gsang gtam dgra bos go song

ਫ ਫ ਫ ਫ ਫ

Heart-talk's not for parents,
It's for an old friend. But –
My love has many stags.
Foes have learned my secrets.

30

snying thub yid 'phrog lha mo
rngon pa rang gis zin kyang
dbang chen mi yi dpon po
nor bzang rgyal bus 'phrogs song

ཪ ཪ ཪ ཪ ཪ

Yidtrok Hlamo – lover –
Though I – the hunter – caught,
Mighty Lord, Prince Norzang,
Seduced my love away.

31

nor bu rang la yod dus
nor bu'i nor nyams ma chod
nor bu mi la shor dus
snying rlung stod la tshangs byung

ཆ ཆ ཆ ཆ ཆ

When I had the jewel,
I prized it not a jot.
When lost to another,
Depression broke my health.

32

rang la dga' ba'i byams pa
gzhan la mdun mar blangs song
khong nang sems pa'i gcong gis
lus po'i sha yang bskams song

ཆ ཆ ཆ ཆ ཆ

My love, who admired me,
Has married another.
Misery gnaws the heart –
My flesh too has dried up.

33

snying thub rku la shor song
mo phywa rtsis 'bul ran song
bu mo gdung sems can ma
rmi lam nang la 'khor song

ཛ ཛ ཛ ཛ ཛ

My love was lost through theft –
Time to consult the cards.
For that passionate girl
Roams round within my dreams.

34

bu mor 'chi ba med na
chang la 'dzad pa mi 'dug
gzhon pa'i gtan gyi skyabs gnas
'di la bcol bas los chog

ছ ছ ছ ছ ছ

If the girl doesn't die
The beer will never stop.
Indeed, I can name her
A young man's safe haven.

35

bu mo a mar ma skyes
kham bu'i shing la skyes sam
a gsar zad pa kham bu'i
me tog de las mgyogs pa

ཆ ཆ ཆ ཆ ཆ

The girl is not human.
Perhaps from a peach tree?
She is ever turning,
Faster than peach flowers.

36

bu mo chung 'dris byams pa
spyang ki'i rigs rgyud min nam
sha 'dris lpags 'dris byung yang
ri la yar grabs mdzad kyis

ছ ছ ছ ছ ছ

That girl, love from childhood.
Does she not spring from wolves?
She sucks my flesh, my skin —
Yet ever plans for peaks.

37

rta rgod ri la rgyab pa
rnyi dang zhags pas zin gyis
byams pa ngo log rgyab pa
mthu ngo zin pa mi 'dug

ཆ ཆ ཆ ཆ ཆ

A wild horse roaming peaks
Can be snared or lassoed.
A lover, rebelling,
Even charms will not hold.

38

brag dang rlung po bsdebs nas
rgod po'i sgro la gzan byung
g.yo can rdzu bag can gyis
nga la gzan po byas byung

ཚ ཚ ཚ ཚ ཚ

Crag and storm united,
To ravage vulture's plumes.
I feel just devoured
By those who plot and plan.

39

sprin pa kha ser gting nag
sad dang se ra'i gzhi ma
ban de skya min ser min
sangs rgyas bstan pa'i dgra bo

ཆ ཆ ཆ ཆ ཆ

Yellow skin, black within,
The cloud yields frost and hail.
Sage not grey, nor saffron –
Such is Buddhism's foe.

40

sa de kha zhu gting 'khyags
rta pho gtong sa ma red
gsar 'grogs byams pa'i phyogs su
snying gtam bshad sa ma red

ཆ ཆ ཆ ཆ ཆ

Frozen ground, surface slips –
No place to send a horse.
A lover newly caught
Is no place for heart-talk.

41

tshes chen bco lnga'i zla ba
yin pa 'dra ba 'dug ste
zla ba'i dkyil gyi ri bong
tshe zad tshar nas 'dug go

ཆ ཆ ཆ ཆ ཆ

What a wonderful time!
It seems like the full moon.
But the man in the moon –
He is going to die.

42

zla ba ’di nas phar ’gro
rting ma’i zla ba tshur yong
bkra shis zla ba dkar po’i
zla stod phyogs la mjal yong

ཆ ཆ ཆ ཆ ཆ

This month has departed,
The next month comes hither.
We meet in the bright part,
Of the lucky white moon.

43

dbus kyi ri rgyal lhun po
ma 'gyur brtan par bzhugs dang
nyi ma zla ba'i bskor phyogs
nor yong bsam pa mi 'dug

ཚ ཚ ཚ ཚ ཚ

Meru, king of mountains –
Centre – don't change, stay firm!
Unthinkable is fault
In sun and moon's orbit.

44

tshes gsum zla ba dkar ba
dkar gos nang nas chod song
bco lnga'i nam dang mnyam pa'i
zhal bzhes cig kyang gnang zhu

ཆ ཆ ཆ ཆ ཆ

The three-day moon is bright,
Completely clothed in white.
Please, will you promise me
Time just like the full-moon?

45

sa bcu'i dbyings su bzhugs pa'i
dam can rdo rje chos skyong
mthu dang nus pa yod na
bstan pa'i dgra bo sgrol dang

ཛ ཛ ཛ ཛ ཛ

O Dharma Protector,
Ten-stage-dwelling, pledge-bound,
Dorje – if strong, able –
Please free the Teaching's foes.

46

khu byug mon nas yong bas
gnam lo'i sa bcud 'phel song
nga dang byams pa phrad nas
lus sems lhod por langs song

ཆ ཆ ཆ ཆ ཆ

The cuckoo comes from Mern,
The year's sap increases.
I and my love have met,
Body and mind relax.

47

skye 'gro mi rtag 'chi ba
snying nas ma dran zer na
spyang grung 'dzoms mdog kha yang
don la lkugs pa 'dra byung

ছ ছ ছ ছ ছ

If you say you don't heed
Change, or death (and mean it),
You may seem smart and wise,
But – strewth! – are like a fool.

48

khyi de stag khyi gzig khyi
ldag kha ster nas 'dris song
nang gi stag mo ral 'dzoms
'dris nas mthu ru langs song

ཆ   ཆ   ཆ   ཆ   ཆ

Tiger-dog; leopard-dog –
A dog – with meat, is tamed.
Long-maned indoor-tigress –
Once known, became more fierce.

49

sha 'jam lus po 'dris kyang
byams pa'i gdeng tshod mi lon
sa la ri mo bris pas
nam mkha'i skar tshod thig byung

ঝ ঝ ঝ ঝ ঝ

Drawing plans on the earth,
I can surmise the stars.
Though I know her soft flesh,
I can't measure her mood.

50

nga dang byams pa'i sdebs sa
lho rong ljon pa'i nags gseb
smra mkhan ne tso ma gtogs
su dang gang gis mi shes
smra mkhan ne tso o shes
gsang kha mdo la ma gnang

ཚ ཚ ཚ ཚ ཚ

The scene of our meeting
Is a southern forest.
It is known by no one,
Save a talking parrot.
Please, O Talking Parrot,
Do not tell my secret.

51

lha sa mi tshogs mthug la
'phyongs rgyas mi spus dag pa
nga la yod pa'i chung 'dris
'phyongs rgyas gzhung la yod do

ཆ ཆ ཆ ཆ ཆ

Lhasa is crowded. Still,
Chongyay has nice people.
That girl, mine from childhood,
Is from its very midst.

52

khyi rgan rgya bo zer ba
rnam shes mi las spyang ba
srod la langs song ma zer
tho rangs log byung ma zer

ཆ ཆ ཆ ཆ ཆ

Old dog – 'Whiskers', he's called –
More sly than a human.
Don't call: 'He left at dusk'.
Don't call: 'He's back at dawn'.

53

srod la byams pa btsal bas
tho rangs kha ba bab byung
gsang dang ma gsang mi 'dug
zhabs rjes gangs la bzhag yod

ཪ ཪ ཪ ཪ ཪ

I sought my love at dusk;
Snow had fallen at dawn.
Why bother with secrets?
– Footprints left in the snow!

54

po ta la ru bzhugs dus
rig 'dzin tshangs dbyangs rgya mtsho
lha sa zhol du sdod dus
'chal po dwangs bzang dbang po

ཚ ཚ ཚ ཚ ཚ

In Potala dwelling –
Rigdzin Tsangyang Gyatso.
Lhasa and Zhol roaming –
Screwer Dangzang Wangbo!

55

sha 'jam mal sa nang gi
snying thub gdung sems can ma
o lo'i rgyu nor 'phrog pa'i
g.yo sgyu bshad pa min 'gro

ཆ ཆ ཆ ཆ ཆ

With soft flesh waits in bed
My passionate lover.
But maybe she deceives
The young lad of his wealth?

56

dbu zhwa dbu la bzhes song
dbu lcang rgyab la dbyugs song
ga ler phebs shig byas pas
ga ler bzhugs shig gsung gis
thugs sems skyo yong byas pas
mgyogs po 'phrad yong gsungs byung

ཆ ཆ ཆ ཆ ཆ

The hat was on her head;
The pigtail down her back.
'Farewell', he said to her,
'Goodbye', was her response.
'I'll miss you', he told her,
'We'll meet soon', she replied.

57

bya de khrung khrung dkar mo
nga la gshog rtsal gyar dang
thag ring rgyang la mi 'gro
li thang bskor nas slebs yong

ཆ ཆ ཆ ཆ ཆ

O bird there – white crane – come,
Lend the strength of your wings.
I'll not go far. Circling
Lithang, I shall return.

58

shi de dmyal ba'i yul gyi
chos rgyal las kyi me long
'di na khrig khrig mi 'dug
de nas khrig khrig gnang zhu

ཚ ཚ ཚ ཚ ཚ

Dead – the mirror of deeds,
Held by the King of Hell.
Here, it's just not been right;
Once there, please make it so.

59

mda' mo 'ben la phog song
mde'u sa la 'dzul song
chung 'dris byams pa 'phrad byung
sems nyid rjes la 'brangs song

ཆ ཆ ཆ ཆ ཆ

The arrow was spot-on,
Its head was in the ground.
Met my love from childhood –
And my heart followed on.

60

rgya gar shar gyi rma bya
kong yul mthil gyi ne tso
'khrungs sa 'khrungs yul mi gcig
'dzoms sa chos 'khor lha sa

ছ ছ ছ ছ ছ

A peacock from Bengal;
Parrot from far Gongbo.
True, their roots differ; but
Holy Lhasa they meet.

61

mi tshos nga la lab pa
dgongs su dag pa khag theg
o lo'i gom gsum phra mo
gnas mo'i nang la thal song

ཚ ཚ ཚ ཚ ཚ

Folk gossip about me.
Sorry – yes, I'm to blame!
A lad's three tiptoe steps –
Oh – I've reached the brothel!

62

lcang ma byi ’ur sems shor
byi ’u lcang mar sems shor
sems shor mthun pa byung na
skya khra hor pas mi thub

ཆ ཆ ཆ ཆ ཆ

The willow loves birdling,
The birdling loves willow.
When love is mutual,
The grey hawk has no chance.

63

da lta'i tshe thung 'di la
de kha tsam zhig zhus nas
rting ma byis pa'i lo la
mjal 'dzom e yong blta'o

ছ ছ ছ ছ ছ

In this short present life,
We have had just so much.
Let's see whether we meet
In our next childhood's years.

64

bya de smra mkhan ne tso
kha rog bzhugs rogs mdzod dang
lcang gling a lce 'jol mo
gsung snyan skyur dgos byas byung

ཆ ཆ ཆ ཆ ཆ

Bird, O Talking Parrot –
Please help, do be silent!
Your sister, Willow Thrush –
Assents to sing sweet songs.

65

rgyab kyi klu bdud btsan po
'jigs dang mi 'jigs mi 'dug
mdun gyi ka ra ku shu
'thogs su dgos pa byas song

ཆ་ ཆ་ ཆ་ ཆ་ ཆ་

Mighty serpent-demon –
He's behind. But who cares!
The sweet apple's in front.
Yes, I think I shall pluck.

66

dang po ma mthong chog pa
sems pa shor don mi 'dug
gnyis pa ma 'dris chog pa
sems gcong yong don mi 'dug

ཆ ཆ ཆ ཆ ཆ

First, better not to see –
Falling in love's senseless.
Second, better not know –
Misery's senseless too.

ᢧ ᢧ ᢧ ᢧ ᢧ

Notes for Appreciation

1

The disc of the full-moon is a common image in Indo-Tibetan
literature for the woman and her face (see especially verse 41, but also
42 and 44). But there is a problem with the expression 'unborn-
mother' (*ma skyes a ma*) here. What does it refer to? Sorensen, in his
commentary on this verse observes that *a ma* (mother) is also a pet-
name in Tibetan for a young woman.[1] That does not explain the
'unborn' (*ma skyes*) though. He notes in passing that there may be a
connection here with the Buddhist philosophy of Madhyamaka that
holds that all things are lacking in intrinsic existence and are thus,
from the point of view of true existence, unreal and therefore
unborn. I want to expand on this point, to provide a possible reading.
Let us speak of level (i) as the level of straightforwardly erotic
meaning. Level (ii) is the level of philosophical understanding.
Then, at level (i) the expression 'unborn mother' refers to the young
woman, perhaps as mother of future unborn children. But at level
(ii), I suggest, it is possible that 'unborn mother' refers to the
goddess Prajñāpāramitā ('Perfection of Wisdom'). This goddess is
frequently referred to in Mahāyāna Buddhism as the 'mother of all
the Buddhas'.[2] She is the personification both of wisdom (*prajñā*)
itself, and also of that which is seen by the mind of wisdom. This is
the ultimate nature of things, emptiness (*śūnyatā*), the complete
absence of true, intrinsic existence. Thus Prajñāpāramitā is the
mother of the unborn, or the mother that indicates the unborn
nature of things. All these references to Madhyamaka philosophy
would have been well known to the Dalai Lama, since it is the

official philosophy of his own dGe lugs pa school.³ But there is more to support this reading. In Tantric Buddhism, also familiar to him from his wider context, *prajñā* is sometimes related to the symbol of the moon. One can see this, for example, in commentaries on the *Guhyasamāja Tantra*, a key text in dGe lugs practice.⁴ Finally, the greatest Indian commentator on Madhyamaka philosophy is also lunar, Candrakīrti (literally, 'Renown of the Moon', in Tibetan Zla ba grags pa, pronounced 'Dawa Drakpa'). Thus, it seems to me, it is plausible that the reference to 'unborn mother' on level (ii) is to wisdom (*prajñā*). But why is Tsangyang Gyatso including this reference here? I do not hold the view that his other verses *all* contain hidden references to Buddhist ideas, beyond their level (i) interpretations. Perhaps the Dalai Lama included the reference here just for the fun of it, to show he could compose a verse of this sort. It would not require an extensive intellectual understanding of Madhyamaka, and the level of practical experience could be nil. Or perhaps the Dalai Lama included this verse at the beginning of his collection precisely to give his critics who may read the verses something to think about. It would suggest to those who bothered to look that really his verses were about Madhyamaka and Tantra, not about maidens and trysts. Or maybe this verse is not by Tsangyang Gyatso at all, but by someone else and has been placed here later – again, perhaps to persuade the reader of symbolic rather than sexual readings of these 'scandalous' verses. Who knows?

Finally, note the use of 'circled' with reference to the face of the young woman. The Tibetan here (*'khor ...*), repeated twice in the original, perhaps carries a hint of threat. It relates to the expression used in Tibetan for *saṃsāra*, 'cyclic existence' (*'khor ba*), the round of death and rebirth. The Dalai Lama knows perfectly well that from a Buddhist point of view sex is threatening.

2

Here I have deliberately adopted a variant reading *rwa co'i gzhu las gyong ba* – 'firmer than a horn bow'. Sorensen considers this reading to be equally plausible. The Dalai Lama is reputed to have enjoyed archery with his friends, and a bow made of yak's horn provides a more vivid image of strength and tautness than the more common reading of *lho gzhu de las gyong ba* – 'firmer than a southern bow'. I have also translated *rgas pa'i lus po*, literally 'body with age', or 'body which has aged', as 'body, growing'. This is a bit loose, but I wanted to capture the erotic sense of the young man's body growing firmer, also linked at this point to the colloquial English sense of 'horn'. However, note that in a Buddhist context there is a sense here also of the young man getting older and therefore heading towards inevitable old age and death. 'Old age' in the Buddhist context is given in Tibetan as well using *rga/rgas*. The expression *gyong ba* (which I have translated as 'firmer') can also carry with it here a sense of 'stiffer', as well as 'harder', 'stronger' and 'tougher'.

3

In Indo-Tibetan culture the ocean is often thought of as a repository of fabulous jewels and other riches, protected by *nāgas*, serpents.

4

The 'love met in passing' is met on the path. But this need not be taken as necessarily a casual affair. She is, after all, a 'lover' (*snying thub*). Tibetans are very fond of turquoises, and there are elaborate classifications of them. Most previous translators have taken it that the turquoise referred to here is of an inferior type. Sorensen argues at length and convincingly that actually the reverse is the case. If so, this reinforces the contention that there is no implication here of a casual, promiscuous sort of affair.

5

The object of the Dalai Lama's affections here is not just the girl (*bu mo*) of the previous poem, met in passing on the path. It is a 'Lady', the daughter of a socially distinguished family. The use of the English 'Lord' here is intended as an approximate equivalent. Her social status is indicated by his bestowal on her of a Tibetan honorific expression (*sras mo*).

The peach is a rare and exciting luxury in Tibet. It has an unblemished soft, smooth, downy fair skin. At least, this one does. It is beautifully curved with exciting and suggestive indentations. This peach has sweet and sensuous juices. She is firm yet yielding, ripe and meet for plucking. But she is a peach just out of reach.

Or perhaps not, if you are a Dalai Lama.

Actually, the only lover of the Sixth Dalai Lama of whom we know the details was indeed such an aristocratic peach. She was a daughter of the Regent of Tibet himself. We do not know if this poem refers to her. But if so, then her apparent unavailability was social and political rather than personal.[5] Perhaps it was religious too. The Dalai Lama, at least when a monk, was normally supposed to be a celibate. But from what we know it seems the young woman herself (honorific or not) needed little encouragement in their relationship.

6

Is this the aristocratic Lady of the previous verse? Since he loses all sleep at night it is implied that he cannot have her at night either. Or does he? Perhaps this is why he loses all sleep.

7

The Dalai Lama appears to consider that falling both in and out of love is as natural and inevitable as the change of the seasons. 'Flowering's time' is essentially the spring, the season *par excellence* for love in Indo-Tibetan literature. Likewise the relationship between the bee and a flower is also a common image of lovers, boy and girl respectively. It looks like the Dalai Lama holds that a bee takes what he needs from the flower. He then leaves it. It is his nature. And the bee is not sad when spring inevitably ends and flowers die. There will be more flowers next year. That is the nature of Nature. The 'fortune of love' in the original suggests the karmic connection that brought the lovers together.

A vivid awareness of impermanence, with its inevitable death, is a central facet of Buddhism. The death of love, as the death of lovers, is nothing to lament. That is just how it is. When karmic causes cease, the results cease too. Seeing it this way is part of 'seeing things the way they really are', an important concept in Buddhist thought.

I wonder if this is really what Tsangyang Gyatso thinks? Or is his ready recourse to a very Buddhist image the natural way for a Dalai Lama to come to terms with a broken heart?

8

A difficult verse to translate. The Tibetan syntax has the grass on the hoarfrost rather than the other way round, and it requires some jiggling to get at the meaning. The use of 'sugars' in the first line is poetic licence on my part. But what the Dalai Lama is saying is clear enough. The pivot of the verse, and its cleverness, lies in its reference to the 'grey yellow storm'. This is the yellow dusty northern wind (*rlung*) of the Tibetan winter.[6] But the Tibetan expression *skya ser*, translated as 'grey yellow' is also used to refer to the Tibetan government, a collaboration of the laity (traditionally thought of as grey (*skya po*) robed) and the saffron or yellow (*ser mo*) robes of the monastic hierarchy. Thus just as the cold winds of winter are what really part the flower and the bee, so the Tibetan political system, the government and the Dalai Lama's place within it, is what truly keeps Tsangyang Gyatso apart from his lover. It is possible also that in using *skya ser* here the Dalai Lama is thinking particularly of the Regent himself, the layman who rules a monastically dominated regime and is thus, as it were, grey *and* yellow (or neither). Compare with verse 39.

If this verse is taken with the previous three verses, perhaps Tsangyang Gyatso's *amour* here is indeed the daughter of the Regent. The powerful Regent is the one who for needs of state truly parts the Dalai Lama from his aristocratic lover. If so, then my suggestion that the resignation of the previous verse represents a Buddhist response to a broken heart gains strength. For clearly in the present verse the Dalai Lama is not so much thinking of the natural ending of all relationships of love because they have run their course. Rather what really parts the two lovers are the cold and unwelcome winter storms of public position, aristocratic and monastic opinion and state power.

9

In Indo-Tibetan poetry the wild goose is the epitome of faithfulness in love. Here, pining for the fens or marshes that are his natural complement, he wants to stay awhile. But now winter has come. All he sees is a sheet of surface ice ('mere ice sheets'). There is nowhere to rest. Tsangyang Gyatso's lover now is cold, oh so cold. She rejects him.

In Tibetan the last line of this poem suggests a state close to despair. The play on the English verb 'to fly away' in this line is not explicit in the Tibetan.

10

As the wooden ferry boat backs away from its mooring it turns to face the current. The horse's head at the prow nods to Tsangyang Gyatso, standing on the shore.[7] Which (it seems) is more than can be said for his brazen (or 'shameless') lover who throws him not a glance as they part. Is this the same aristocratic young woman grown cold of his previous verses? If so, it appears that even if their parting is in response to a Tibetan political system that had come to discourage such a liaison, she shows him no regrets. But what is not shown is not necessarily unfelt.

11

Enough of his aristocratic Lady! It is all too risky, and the pain is too great. Here the Dalai Lama pledges the vows of young lovers with a market girl. There is no use of the Tibetan honorific here. She is a mere *bu mo*. Market girls are rather coarse, low-class creatures with a promiscuous reputation.

What three-word pledge might they twine? Why not 'I love you', 'We shall marry', 'True love forever', 'We shall elope'? No use! None of it is meant. Like a coiled striped snake (*khra bo'i sbrul*) that cannot actually be knotted (*mdud pa ... ma brgyab*), the pledge unravels all by itself and slithers off into the dirty undergrowth. The Tibetan *rang rang sa la* – all by itself – I have translated as 'alone'. This is a bit imprecise and ambiguous as a translation of the Tibetan, but it is intentionally so. I like the idea that a pledge made together unravels not just by itself but also when the lovers have gone their different ways, gone home. Each is now alone. There is nothing to keep them to their vows. It was never meant. How could it be, when one is the Dalai Lama and the other a promiscuous market girl?

Sorensen takes seriously the suggestion by a Chinese writer that the 'market girl' here is an allusion to the Regent. The poem thus makes a veiled political allusion. I find that weird. The same could be said of many similar cases where Sorensen searches for political allusions in his commentary.

12

Lhasa has many willow trees, and like the parks of modern Western cities they are good places for lovers to meet. Perhaps partly for this reason the willow tree also becomes a Tibetan symbol of love. On to such a tree Tsangyang Gyatso has installed prayer flags.

Prayer flags have religious formulae (e.g. *mantras*) on them. They are flown ostensibly in order to remind people of religious aspirations like compassion, and to purify spiritually the environment. Flying such flags creates religious merit. A good follower of Mahāyāna will offer the merit accrued for the benefit of all sentient beings. But in practice one can offer the merit to, for example, one's lady friend. Effectively therefore, flying prayer flags can be used to bring good fortune (through transference of merit) to a named individual.

These prayer flags are there in order to bring good fortune to Tsangyang Gyatso's lover. This young woman is not one he has just met. She is a woman he has known from when they were small. Perhaps they grew up together. But among Lhasa officials is a Guardian of Willows. The Dalai Lama politely begs him to keep quiet about it all, and not to throw stones at their prayer flag.

13

Letters written on paper can be washed off. Experiences, memories, the images conjured by the mind, can never be lost even if one tries to hide from them. They are now part of the person one has become. They are always there.

I wonder if the Dalai Lama here weeps at the sight of old love letters?

14

In the first line I have preferred the reading *brgyab* – past tense 'stamped' – to Sorensen's *rgyab*. Sorensen himself considers the past-tense reading possibly a preferable one. Both words are pronounced the same in Tibetan. I have rendered the negation of the Tibetan expression for 'concern' here (i.e. lack of concern) as 'heartless' in translating verse 10. The Tibetan affirmative covers a range of meanings – consideration for others, modesty, decency or sense of shame.

Perhaps, as Sorensen suggests, in this verse the Dalai Lama shows frustration with his official duties, rubber-stamping state documents. In reality the stamp is just plain stupid. There are more important things for intelligent lovers to be stamping than all this paperwork, such as, for example, a sense of care and concern for each other.

I wonder if this poem was written before or after poem 10? Alas for Tsangyang Gyatso, as far as he is concerned the young woman in that verse showed that the stamp had apparently failed to make much imprint.

15

The bee once more seeks the flower. The 'gorgeous hollyhocks' here have in the Tibetan a thousand wonderful petals (*stong ldan ha lo'i me tog*). But Sorensen suggests that the hollyhock had a reputation in Tibet for being a bit 'common' (perhaps in England at springtime, daffodils might be an equivalent). These hollyhocks are to be employed as ritual offerings in the main temple.

But what is the Dalai Lama thinking? Does he really want to be led to the temple in order to buzz round the gorgeous flowers that are being offered there? To pounce on beautiful nuns, or young women at their devotions?

Still, no doubt a bee will do what a bee must do. And it is the hollyhock's fault for looking so gorgeous.

16

It seems that Tsangyang Gyatso's present beloved is indeed keen on her Buddhism. It looks as if she has decided to become a nun (the Tibetan literally says 'going to the Superior Doctrine', i.e. Buddhism, but in context it must mean something like becoming a nun). That is perhaps an appropriate response to becoming the object of the Dalai Lama's affections. After all he was supposed to be a monk. Note here that the sweetheart is given the Tibetan honorific verb (*bzhugs*). The 'young man' is given the equivalent non-honorific verb (*sdod*). Thus the young man here, as elsewhere in the poems, is the author himself.

The Tibetan actually states that he, her 'young man' (*pho gzhon*), will head immediately for a mountain hermitage. Quite how becoming a mountain hermit will help him is not clear. Perhaps he is throwing back at her what she is doing to him. Or perhaps he is genuinely torn between his lust and his religious aspirations and status. If he cannot have her, then that settles it. He will have religion.

Note, incidentally, that the state of a monk or nun in Buddhism is theoretically reversible. Nevertheless reverting to lay life has always been rather frowned upon in Tibet. It is opting for the lesser state of life rather than the greater.

17

Verses like this are lovely. They indicate the very human nature of this Dalai Lama. He goes for spiritual guidance ('holy help' is a loose translation for an expression that is more precise in the Tibetan Buddhist context) to a famous lama, with all the proper qualifications expected of an effective teacher and spiritual guide. All Dalai Lamas have their own gurus. This verse quite possibly refers to approaching his teacher, the Second Panchen Lama. But Tsangyang Gyatso simply cannot concentrate. He cannot meditate. He can hardly begin to apply even the basic teachings of Buddhist mental cultivation. Rather than rapture, he is rapt. Wrapped up in thoughts of his beloved.

Verses like these, which show a great Tibetan religious figure who admits to failure in basic Buddhist practice (here because of his love (or lust) for a young woman), are, I think, unique. They have been preserved precisely because Tsangyang Gyatso *was* the Dalai Lama.

18

Literally the Tibetan speaks of the face of the lama that is being meditated on, and contrasts it with the face of the beloved that is not the object of meditation. In Tibetan Buddhist meditation practice one often visualizes one's own teacher in the form of a Buddha. Visualization must be precise and accurate, as if seeing the Buddha/Guru directly in front of oneself. One need not think (as does Tatz in his note on this verse[8]) that attempting this indicates a particularly advanced familiarity with tantric practice on the part of the Dalai Lama. And unfortunately Tsangyang Gyatso cannot see his teacher's face at all. But he has no problem, sitting there in silence on his meditation cushion, in seeing quite clearly the face of his beloved young woman.

It is strange how when one is asked to visualize a Buddha in meditation it is usually so difficult. Yet it seems so easy to visualize that to which one's mind is strongly attracted. Alas, this is invariably the wrong thing.

19

To become a Buddha in one lifetime (naturally therefore with one body) is the hope and boast of the highest level of tantric practice. Tsangyang Gyatso is here expressing his level of devotion to his love, but he also clearly sees her as the wrong object if he wishes to attain the tantric goal.

20

This is the poem that is always taken to show Tsangyang Gyatso's familiarity with advanced tantric practices, practices that involved engaging in physical sexuality for the purpose of inner spiritual cultivation. Sorensen calls it 'a poem of baffling intricacy'. Dhondup comments that 'this song is purely tantric and partially reveals Tsangyang Gyatso's mastery over tantra'.[9] Sorensen has shown that the references here are primarily to the teachings of the 'Brug pa bKa' brgyud (pronounced 'Drukpa Kagyer') tradition and a particular geographical area of south-eastern Tibet, rather than the Dalai Lama's dGe lugs. The verse refers to the use of alchemical magic.

First, supposing that this verse is genuinely by the Sixth Dalai Lama, what does it show? Well, it might show that the poet Dalai Lama can write what appears to be a 'hymn of tantric experience', like other Tibetan poets such as Mi la ras pa (pronounced 'Milarepa'). This is a particular speciality of the bKa' brgyud schools and goes back to the Indian tantric *dohās* of figures like Saraha and Nāropa. It would show that the Dalai Lama can operate with tantric categories in composing verses. What it would *not* show (*pace* some other Tibetan and modern Western scholars) is that all Tsangyang Gyatso's affairs with women were not what they appeared to be – affairs with women that (as we have seen in previous verses) caused him some emotional turmoil. Verse 20 does not show that really Tsangyang Gyatso's sexual behaviour was part of tantric spiritual practices, rather than simply love affairs. There is no suggestion in the verses that this is actually the case. To try, on the strength of verse 20, to interpret most of the other verses as having a secret tantric significance would be to stretch credulity.

We should note the last two lines. Like so many of Tsangyang Gyatso's verses, the direction of this verse, its whole momentum, is contained at the end. With this marvellous drink those deeds that Buddhists usually hold lead to unfavourable rebirths will no longer do so. My translation refers to hell, as having greater impact in English. The Tibetan, on the other hand, speaks of 'bad destinies', the three classes of negative rebirth as an animal, a hungry ghost or in hell. What is interesting about this verse, therefore, is that the Dalai Lama is clinging to a recipe that will save him from the horrible rebirths that would seem to be contingent upon the sort of behaviour in which he likes to indulge. In particular here it may be drinking alcohol. Or it could be love of women. Either way, in spite of an initial difference, verse 20 is in keeping with the other verses. In the most recent verses the Dalai Lama has turned to religion, but because of his love for his girlfriend he is finding it difficult to practise even basic Buddhist meditation techniques. Had he been able to do so he could have become a Buddha by now. Of course one can become a Buddha in one lifetime by high tantric practice, but Tsangyang Gyatso has realized that his more immediate concern is how to escape unfavourable rebirths. And apparently that requires keeping commitments, with perhaps some alchemical help. 'Commitments' here could be tantric commitments, but could also be simply trust between partners. Sorensen refers to a popular Tibetan use of the last line as a toast when drinking alcohol.[10] Alcohol consumption is very much frowned upon by strict Buddhists.

In recent years enormous advances have been made in coming to appreciate the direction of this verse, if not all its details. Sorensen (relying in part on the work of others) writes a lengthy essay on its interpretation. Essentially this is the bare bones of a medicinal recipe, the product of which is a substance that (it is claimed) leads to supernormal powers. Important here is the power of avoiding bad rebirths. At the time the Sixth Dalai Lama was writing there seems to have been considerable interest in such magical alchemical products in certain influential Tibetan circles. It may be that the alchemical substance referred to here could be added to alcohol in order to make it spiritually potent or to neutralize the spiritual negativity of alcohol consumption. 'Dakpashelri water' is glacier water from Dakpashel ('Pure Crystal') Mountain, an identifiable site in south-eastern Tibet. It is an important area replete with 'mystical topography' for tantric practice, close to where Tsangyang Gyatso was born. It is also a significant region for the practice of Tibetan herbal medicine. 'Luderdorje' ('Serpent-demon Diamond') is an identifiable botanical herb used in Tibetan medicine. The root is apparently related to ginseng. In Chinese (but not Tibetan) medicine it is reputed to be an aphrodisiac. This herb is also associated with potions that (it is said) convey remarkable magical powers (*siddhi*), such as the ability to fly through the air. Tibetan sources refer to the great blessings that come even from drinking the dewdrops that fall from it. Significantly, one Mongolian source (quoted by Sorensen) explains that simply going to the place at Dakpashelri where the herb can be found liberates one from the round of transmigration and from bad rebirths.[11] There is a work attributed to the Sixth Dalai Lama that mentions medicinal elixirs of the type referred to in this verse. In tantric writing a *ḍākinī* is a female demi-goddess (Sorensen: 'enchantress') particularly associated with aiding advanced tantric practitioners. They can also appear as 'ordinary' human women. Here the wisdom-*ḍākinī* serves as a *chang ma*, a 'beer-girl', one of the beautiful females well known at Lhasa parties. It looks like with the use of this marvellous herbal medicine the beer-girl at the party or in the tavern is held to be in fact (or becomes) a *ḍākinī*.

The upshot of all of this is that 'it is evident that we are here dealing with a sacred-occult tradition where ... this herbal plant [Luderdorje] becomes a constituent part, in a medicinal-therapheutic [sic] and alchemical context, of a sacred item which eventually secures the partaker supernatural powers.'[12] Note, however, that while verse 20 shows a familiarity with this product it does not in itself give evidence for any great familiarity on the part of the Dalai Lama with the actual procedure and techniques involved in its manufacture or even its use. Thus, granted the meaning of this verse, it cannot be taken as showing an advanced knowledge on the part of Tsangyang Gyatso of the alchemical tradition involved. All it shows is that he knew of it, and presumably sampled its products in the hope of avoiding nasty rebirths.

21

This young woman is described as bright and charming. She invited the Dalai Lama to her house as a guest. The suggestion is that such good luck befell Tsangyang Gyatso because he had recently set up new prayer flags with the intention of improving his luck. 'With my prayer flags flapping' is a little bit of a loose translation, but the meaning of the Tibetan is caught.

22

In spite of a translation by Sorensen of the first two lines using the first-person singular, the Tibetan does not say specifically that these lines refer to Tsangyang Gyatso looking at a row of young women (at, say, a party). I have chosen to preserve here the ambiguity of the original. It could be (as Dhondup translates, albeit otherwise very loosely) that it is the *young woman* rather than the Dalai Lama who is taking in a whole row with general social smiles, while casting side-long glances of love at Tsangyang Gyatso.

23

The translation is a little less than strictly literal, but it gets the meaning pretty well and I like it.

24

The expression *mdzangs ma*, a charming, bright, clever young woman, suggests that Tsangyang Gyatso is still thinking of the girl of verse 21. The expression *chos skal* refers to the possibilities he has in this life for practising Buddhism. The Dalai Lama is caught in a dilemma. One interesting dimension of this dilemma is the tension between following the wishes of another and going along with one's own wishes and hopes. Of course, in this Buddhist context 'one's own wishes and hopes' refers to one's spiritual growth towards Buddhahood eventually *for the benefit of all sentient beings*. The Dalai Lama is quite clear that opposed to the life of sex, partying, fun and perhaps eventually marriage is the isolated way of a religious hermit in the mountains, acting for the benefit of all sentient beings.

It is hard not to feel that the Dalai Lama has brought this acute dilemma on himself. Still, we need to remember his youth and his unenviable position.

25

Gongbo (Kong po) is a district not far from Lhasa. Presumably the Dalai Lama is thinking of himself and his dilemma in this guise. According to Sorensen, three days is commonly thought of in Tibet to be as long as a casual relationship can last before it becomes something more serious. The 'web' here can also be translated as 'net'. Either way, the bee feels caught and struggles to escape. For the Dalai Lama where could one escape to, but to the serious practice of religion, Buddhism?

26

It is common in Tibet for a lover to give his young woman a turquoise for her head dress. It may even be given as a sign of betrothal. But how is one to know that one's girlfriend's *thoughts* are faithful?

My interpretation of this verse differs rather from that of Sorensen. For comparison, he translates it:

Should you, my eternal friend,
On whom my thoughts have lingered,
Prove just brazen and unfaithful,
The turquoise I have inserted in my hairdress
Would not know how to divulge it to me.

I assume Sorensen must think it is the *young woman* who is speaking in this verse (although he seems to contradict this on p 157 of his edition and commentary). He also takes 'the thoughts' as referring to the speaker's relationship to the beloved. I do not.

27

Rather nicely, the Dalai Lama youth here asks very politely of his lover with the sparkling teeth whether she has 'truly' – from the heart (*snying nas*) – hot flesh (*sha tsha*) for him or not! The second line in the Tibetan rather hints that she is instructing (with 'guidance for his mind', *blo khrid*) as well as seducing him.

28

The first line here is a common Tibetan image for a chance or casual meeting. A bird meets a stone quite adventitiously. It alights on a stone apparently randomly, and a thrown stone just happening to hit a bird would also be quite accidental. The madam here (in the Tibetan) is a lady who dispenses beer. But she also plays a role in bringing casual lovers together, perhaps as an inn-cum-brothel keeper. The Tibetan implies the possibility of unwanted results through *karman* from deeds misdone, as well as punning on 'debt' and 'acquiring a child' (*bu lon*). Hence the translation's 'issue'. Presumably, if this applies to himself, the Dalai Lama is suggesting that if his liaison has issue and his partner becomes pregnant it is the madam who should pay for the upkeep of the child and not him. It is after all quite literally her business. One should also remember that apart from anything else, the Dalai Lama presumably does not wish his liaisons to become common knowledge.

However, with its pun I would see this verse as a joke rather than a genuine attempt to avoid responsibility. After all, as a Buddhist the Dalai Lama knows perfectly well that karmic results can be experienced only by the one who did the deed. Likewise financial (and moral) responsibility for illegitimate births is unlikely to be avoided by those who engendered the 'issue'.

29

The 'old friend' here is in Tibetan a 'love from childhood' (see verse 12). I have used 'friend' for alliterative affect. Even a Dalai Lama – especially a Dalai Lama – cannot know whom he can trust. As all spies are aware, secrets told on pillows can travel far. This Dalai Lama has enemies, and they now know what he is up to.

30

This verse requires a bit of explanation. The allusion is to a Buddhist story originating in India that is well known in Tibet and became the subject of a Tibetan folk-opera. It is outlined by Sorensen in his commentary on this verse. There was a king who ruled righteously because of the advice given him by a *nāga* (a serpent-deity). His neighbouring king, on the other hand, was wicked. The wicked king sent a magician to abduct the nāga. The plot was foiled by a hunter. Out of gratitude, the nāga gave the hunter a magic lasso, quite a useful thing for a hunter. With this lasso the hunter caught a beautiful goddess, Yidtrok Hlamo. He gave the goddess to his prince, Prince Norzang. They lived happily, but Prince Norzang's other consorts, out of jealousy, persuaded the king, Norzang's father, to execute Yidtrok Hlamo and to send the prince off to war. The queen rescued Yidtrok Hlamo, who flew back to the heaven from where she came. Prince Norzang was victorious in battle but upset by developments in his love life. He set out to rescue Yidtrok Hlamo, found her again, and they all lived happily ever after.

Clearly Tsangyang Gyatso has changed the story somewhat. He is the hunter and has successfully trapped his prey. But instead of giving this wonderful female to Prince Norzang, the latter – a horrible, powerful aristocrat – has stolen her from him. In the Tibetan there is an interesting repetition of 'phrog (pronounced 'trok') in the name of Yidtrok Hlamo and in the verb in the last line that I have translated as 'seduced'. The name Yidtrok Hlamo literally means 'Mind-captivating Goddess' (as it is aptly translated by Sorensen). The 'phrog is the 'captivating' part. Just as she is a goddess who, through her beauty, captivates the mind, so in the Dalai Lama's version she has been stolen ('captured') by Prince Norzang. Yet human beings are not inanimate possessions, property. In that sense they cannot simply be 'stolen' (at least, not in love). They must in some sense give themselves. Thus I have used 'seduced' instead, a word that also has a much better impact here.

An alternative translation, playing on the names of the protagonists, might be fun. *Yidtrok Hlamo*, as a name, essentially means that the goddess is very beautiful (with a beauty that has a certain otherworldly magical enticing power). In English we might call her 'Divine'. *Norzang* means literally in Tibetan 'good wealth'. In effect he is Prince Jolly Rich. So let us try:

> She – 'Divine' – my lover –
> Though I – the hunter – caught,
> Strong Lord, Prince Jolly Rich,
> Seduced my love away.

This does perhaps get some of the additional sense that Tsangyang Gyatso is trying to convey with this verse – the young woman's beauty and also (in the way he has twisted the story) his attitude to the aristocratic seducer. I wonder who these two were? One would imagine the 'Mighty Lord, Prince Norzang' must be the Regent, who also enjoyed ladies and could claim reasons of statecraft for his seduction.

31

On this verse see the Appendix, *The Mind of a Dalai Lama*.

32

The Tibetan in the first line literally says 'love who took joy in me'. The illness referred to in Tibetan in the third line is described as a chronic disease of the mind that is located or emerges from deep within. In the Appendix below I note the association in Tibetan medicine of bodily wasting with the particular psychophysical illness that, it seems to me, was experienced by the Sixth Dalai Lama. Tatz's translation, '[t]he flesh of my body is dry' makes it sound like Tsangyang Gyatso suffered from flaky skin or eczema. That misses it.

33

Where is she? Does he still have a chance? Are their futures linked in the stars? In losing her Tsangyang Gyatso has become obsessed with this young woman. In my discussion in the Appendix it will be noted that insomnia is also one of the symptoms listed for disorders of what Tibetan medicine calls 'the pervasive wind'. The verse actually refers to divination and astrology. I have used 'cards' as a common Western equivalent. In Tibet there are many forms of divination that are a constant accompaniment of everyday living for everyone from the Dalai Lama down.[13]

34

An interesting verse, since it rather skilfully plays on Buddhist themes. The young woman here is presumably a beer-girl, although she may also be his lover. Buddhism of course stresses impermanence and consequential suffering. What the Dalai Lama wants to say is that *if* the beer-girl never dies, there will be beer forever. He is the Dalai Lama. He permits himself to appoint her the 'safe haven' (actually in Tibetan, 'firm' or 'constant refuge'; *gtan gyi skyabs gnas*) of the young man (or 'young men'). The Tibetan expression *skyabs gnas* is precisely the term used when 'taking refuge' in the Buddha, the Doctrine (*Dharma*) and the community of practitioners (*Saṃgha*). This is the basic practice expressing Buddhist adherence. Thus the Dalai Lama is here taking refuge not in Buddha, Dharma and Saṃgha, but in a beer-girl. In a way it is a wicked – even blasphemous – joke. But it is tinged with sadness and Buddhist truth. We know that in fact the beer-girl will die. She is not in reality a safe refuge. The young man Tsangyang Gyatso might love women and beer, but he knows that all will pass away, and its passing (as Buddhism constantly stresses) is misery.

35

Literally, the first line states that perhaps she was not born from a mother. Peach blossom is beautiful but very temporary. In Japan the reference would be to cherry blossom, although for Japanese to compare a lover to cherry blossom would be a positive feature even if tinged with the sadness of mortality. Here, perhaps the Dalai Lama wants to emphasize his lover's fickleness or changeability rather more than her beauty. This is particularly the case if we take this verse with those that follow.

36

The Tibetan verb does not translate literally as 'sucks', but this translation gets the dual meaning of what a wolf and a young woman may each do to Tsangyang Gyatso, given half a chance. A nearer translation would be 'knew' with its erotic Biblical sense included. It seems Tsangyang Gyatso's lover is a loner, unwilling to make a commitment. He is devoured, but she is always planning to go off alone to the mountains. She sounds in many ways like Tsangyang Gyatso himself. I wonder if this is the same young woman who intended to become a nun?

37

Tsangyang Gyatso *is* the Dalai Lama. The reference to rebellion in this verse is a potent one. The Tibetan *mthu* ('charms') expresses here magical power. Nothing can hold back a lover who bids for freedom.

38

Even a soaring mountain vulture (we might prefer the image of an eagle) can be ground down by the weather and by the jagged crags of the Himalayas. And the Dalai Lama feels *devoured* by the secret whisperings, the secret schemings, with which he is surrounded.

39

A complicated poem to interpret. The reference in the third line is to a learned scholar (*ban de*) who is neither a layman wearing grey robes nor a monk in saffron-yellow. The Dalai Lama's poem here is perhaps directed at the Regent of Tibet (see my comments on verse 8 above), who was a very learned layman occupying the position of a ruler who should have been a monk, the Dalai Lama himself. Or is the Dalai Lama (or someone) here referring with regret to the Dalai Lama himself, suspended between his monastic status and his lay preferences?[14]

40

One had better not talk intimately or tell secrets to a new girlfriend. We saw in verse 29 that even an old love known for many years can betray such confidences. A new girlfriend is like ground that is frozen underneath and slippery on the surface. It is very dangerous. No place to send one's horse. If the horse falls on the hazardous surface or one is unseated, on the exposed steppes one can freeze to death at night. The Tibetan indicates that the horse here is a stallion (*rta pho*). The suggestion is that to speak confidences to a new girlfriend would be a highly risky business. Who is there that can be trusted?

41

What a wonderful verse! The Tibetan refers to the 'moon of the fifteenth day', that is, the full moon. A full moon is a common image in Indo-Tibetan arts for love (or sometimes the young woman or her face; see verse 1). Also common here is the 'man in the moon'. But with a difference. In India and Tibet it is not a man who is seen in the shadows on the moon's disc. It is a much loved hare (*ri bong*).

And so it is in this verse too. The Tibetan actually reads 'But the hare on the moon's disc is going to die'. On the colloquial future sense of the last line, see Sorensen. Of course, as the moon wanes ('perishes') the man, or the hare, too will perish. Again we see a particular streak of pessimism in the Dalai Lama, especially regarding uncertainty and impermanence, which perhaps reflects his Buddhism. But we have also seen that some of this pessimism is justified. The Dalai Lama's anxiety perhaps reflects his upbringing and early experiences (see the Appendix).

And all love ends in death. So maybe this is not pessimism but realism. The Dalai Lama is concerned (or perhaps recognizes) that his love is doomed to perish. But does he also see himself in the hare? Can one see Tsangyang Gyatso's premonition of his destiny?

42

The Tibetan in this verse is able to pun on 'moon' and 'month', for in Tibetan they are the same word (*zla ba*). The time of the waxing moon is known as the bright part, or bright half, and it is harbinger of the auspicious white moon. The time of the waxing moon is just the time for lovers to meet. And that, the verse says, is indeed when they shall meet. As Sorensen points out, compared with the previous verse this has an optimistic note. But all waxing moons eventually wane. Remembering that the moon is a symbol of love and the lover, all growing love eventually perishes (as does the lover). Or, to change to another image favoured by Tsangyang Gyatso, the turquoise bee moves on to other flowers (see verse 7).

43

In Indo-Tibetan cosmology Mount Meru is the central cosmic mountain of the universe (a 'world-sphere'). The rotation of the sun and the moon takes place around it.[5] The Dalai Lama is clearly exhorting someone, or something, to remember its status as the firm centre of all. It is unthinkable that there would be deviation in the rotation of others around him/her/it. Their orbit is their very nature. Apart from that, who knows what this verse is about? Sorensen suggests various possibilities. I rather doubt any particular allusion to tantric yoga here, even though these cosmic symbols are used there too. Mount Meru in this verse could be Tsangyang Gyatso's lover, around whom he dances. Or the other way round. Or perhaps the reference here is not to his lover, but to political figures such as the Regent. The Dalai Lama is, after all, the Dalai Lama and thus supposedly the firm centre of Tibet. But then, who is dancing around whom? Anyway, *someone* or *something* should stay firm and unmoving.

44

The three-day moon is that of the third day of the waxing half. We are still far from the full moon. As Sorensen points out, there is a pun at the end of this verse. The Tibetan *zhal* in the last line – related here to an expression for promising – is also a term for the face. Thus (remembering the association of the moon with love, and also the lover's face), Tsangyang Gyatso is asking that she show to him her full face, as at the time of the full moon. The time for the third day of the waxing moon is fun, but full-moon time is even better.

45

See my comments on this verse in 'The present translation' section of the Introduction.

46

A cuckoo is a harbinger or a symbol of spring, and in Indian and Tibetan literature that is the season for lovers. Thus to mention a cuckoo is to contribute to the mood (Sanskrit: *rasa*) of amorous enjoyment. The cuckoo returns to Lhasa from its winter migration to the southern regions of Mern (Mon) in the sub-Himalayas. The sap (literally, the 'earth-essence'; Sorensen: 'fertility') is rising. The Tibetan suggests that it is *because* the cuckoo has arrived that all this is happening. Sorensen cites another Tibetan verse (not by the Sixth Dalai Lama) that explains that this is due to the cuckoo's beautiful song.

This is a lovely, sensuous verse, written very much in the style of a Sanskrit love poem but (it seems) with greater directness in the last line. One can almost feel Tsangyang Gyatso's relaxation of tension.

Of course, winter will certainly come again.

47

A very Buddhist sentiment. Actually this verse has much of the flavour of the Indian poet Bhartṛhari's *Vairāgyaśataka* ('Hundred Verses on Renunciation'), particularly as Bhartṛhari too was torn between the sensuous life of love and the religious life of asceticism and meditation.[16] Nevertheless one has to admit that this poem seems rather out of keeping with most of the others. I wonder whether it is really by Tsangyang Gyatso? It is not included in some of the other recensions.

48

Literally, the last line says that she became even stronger. 'Tiger-dogs' and 'leopard-dogs' are just horribly fierce dogs. But not as dangerous as long-haired domestic tigresses. The Tibetan verb is the same in the second and fourth lines. I have chosen 'known' in the last line intentionally, with the implications it has of its erotic usage for 'carnal knowledge' in the King James Bible.

49

Translation lines a/b and c/d are reversed in the original Tibetan (i.e. the reference to the young woman comes first), which does not seem poetically as effective. The translation of 'mood' for *gdeng* is a bit imprecise. The Tibetan conveys the sense of 'confidence' or 'assurance'.

50

The talking parrot is associated with the south of Tibet, on the borders with India. The region is known as Hlorong (Lho rong), and the Tibetan describes the meeting deep in a forest in a Hlorong valley. Sorensen suggests that this verse might be aimed at someone in the Dalai Lama's entourage who had come to hear of his master's secret liaison.

51

Chongyay ('Phyongs rgyas) is south of Lhasa and close to the valley from where the ancient Tibetan kings emerged in the seventh century to conquer briefly much of Central Asia and China. The Tibetan expression (with its double ... *la yod* construction) rather suggests that 'this girl is mine, yet she *lives* elsewhere'.

52

Is this an actual guard dog, or a member of the Dalai Lama's household?

53

This verse is, I think, self-explanatory. It is a masterpiece, with all the crispness of a zen haiku.

54

The Potala is the Dalai Lama's great palace that towers over Lhasa. Zhol is the area at the foot of the Potala that contains (inter alia) the red-light district. The Dalai Lama's name, Tsangyang Gyatso, has a number of translations. It could mean 'The Ocean, Purity and Harmony', or 'The Ocean, Perfection and Harmony', or 'The Ocean, Pure Harmony', or 'The Ocean, Perfect Harmony', or 'The Ocean, Harmony [or 'Melody'] of the god Brahmā'. Whichever, the Dalai Lama's name is replete with intimations of perfection, good-ness and beauty. The title *Rigdzin* is used to refer to one who is a tantric master. However, Sorensen argues that the bestowal of this title on the Sixth Dalai Lama need not be taken to mean that he was thought to be an accomplished practitioner of esoteric Tantra. In fact it was also applied to the father of Tsangyang Gyatso,[17] who was not reputed for his tantric accomplishments as far as I know.

The Tibetan *'chal po*, which I have translated as 'Screwer', means literally an adulterer or someone who is exceptionally promiscuous.

The Dalai Lama's name as a libertine is Dangzang Wangbo. 'Dang-zang' (*dwangs bzang*) when used colloquially, as it is here, is a term which when applied to a male means 'handsome'. 'Wangbo' (*dbang po*) normally means 'powerful', but here Sorensen suggests that it should be translated as 'potent'. Thus the Dalai Lama is known in the red-light district as 'The Screwer, Handsome and Potent'.

Sorensen also points out that the verb in the first line ('dwelling') is an honorific. That in the third line, which I translate here as 'roaming', is not. Since it is not normal to use an honorific for oneself, Sorensen suggests that while this verse may sum up the career of the Sixth Dalai Lama, it is probably not actually by him. I am not convinced. In the Introduction I suggest another reason why the Dalai Lama might have used these two versions of the verb for poetic effect.

55

The Tibetan expression 'wealth' (*rgyu nor*) here has a variant *dge nor*, 'precious virtue'. Adopting this variant, the last line would read ' The young lad of his virtue'. That would give an interesting alternative.

56

This is not an easy verse to translate because of the infrequent use of personal pronouns in literary Tibetan. Thus we cannot be sure who is speaking to whom. All we can tell is that the third line is ad-dressed to the person leaving, and the fourth line to the one remaining. Tibetan uses a different expression when speaking to each. Moreover, since the Sixth Dalai Lama on renouncing his monastic vows grew his hair long, we do not know whether the second line refers to him or to his girlfriend. I have translated it one way, but others are possible. My translation relies on the assumption that the one leaving is the young woman. This is based on the one leaving wearing the hat, and the use of an honorific for the hat wearer in the first line. The Dalai Lama is the poet, and he would not be expected to use an honorific for himself. Sorensen, while recognizing the possibility of translating the verse the way I favour, differs. He wants the last line to be the Dalai Lama speaking, in

order to link it with the next verse. I see no need to do so. Either
way, the poem is a lovely evocation of parting lovers which gains by
its simplicity.

My use of 'I'll miss you' in the fifth line is a little loose. The
Tibetan simply says that there will be sorrow, or weariness.

57

This is a well-known and popular verse, mainly because it is taken to
be a prediction of the Dalai Lama's reincarnation. Its authenticity
can be doubted. The white crane is a symbol of longevity and
fidelity. Lithang is in the far east of Tibet, on the Chinese border.
The Seventh Dalai Lama was born in that region in 1708.

58

The king of hell is the ancient Indian god Yama. He is described in
the Tibetan as *Chos rgyal*, Sanskrit *Dharmarāja*, the King of
Dharma. *Dharma* in this context in Buddhism combines the two
notions of the way things really are, and the way they ought to be in
one's behaviour if one is to correspond (as one should) to the way
things actually are.[18] It might best be thought of here as something
akin to 'righteousness'. In Buddhism Yama holds up a mirror in
which one can see exactly one's deeds and their consequences. Thus
properly speaking Yama does not judge the dead person. That person
is judged with perfect fairness and justice by the inevitable results of
the deeds he has committed. This vision of moral truth takes place
not strictly in hell but in a sort of antechamber. There is no impli-
cation that in looking into the mirror of deeds one will inevitably
proceed to hell. But if one does, in Buddhism there are many hells.
They are all jolly unpleasant. Still, hell is not for all eternity. It is a
kind of rebirth, where one exhausts the results of one's wicked deeds.
Then there is rebirth elsewhere. When further wicked deeds are
committed, hell may result again. And so on, forever – unless one
becomes enlightened and puts a stop to the whole cyclic treadmill.

According to Sorensen this verse often ends recensions of the
Sixth Dalai Lama's poems. In the previous verse he predicted his
reincarnation. Now he speaks of his after-death quest for justice.

59

Tsangyang Gyatso was by all accounts an accomplished archer himself.[19] The arrow here is said to have hit the target (*'ben la phog song*). Important here is that arrows are also used in Tibet as a form of divination.[20]

60

The peacock is said here to come from eastern India (*rgya gar shar*). Since our peacock is in Lhasa, it is more likely to come from north-eastern India, i.e. Bengal. For Gongbo see verse 25. Lhasa is described here as *chos 'khor*, the *Dharmacakra*, Dharma-circle or Dharma-wheel. This refers to a place particularly holy for Buddhism. Two creatures – symbols of lovers – from quite different origins meet here, at a third place, the enchanted city of Lhasa.

61

The *gnas mo* ('landlady') of this verse is probably like the *a ma chang ma* of verse 28. She is the keeper of an inn-cum-brothel, a madam. This verse takes us to her place. I do not see any reason to think that the lady *herself* is the Dalai Lama's mistress (as Sorensen suggests).

62

'The birdling' is in the Tibetan a 'little bird' (*byi 'u*). It may be the small willow sparrow. So long as it nestles deep within the willow branches it might be safe. The Tibetan *sems shor* literally means 'lost its mind/heart [to]'. Sorensen suggests that the 'grey hawk' (*skya khra hor pa*) is perhaps a sparrowhawk or falcon. Etymologically, Tibetans associate it with Mongolia (*hor yul*).

63

A verse that manages to combine a certain depression with hope for the future, if only in a future incarnation. There is an issue in Buddhist philosophy as to how far my reincarnation can be said to be 'me'. But no doubt such philosophical niceties are far from the Dalai Lama's mind.

64

The parrot should shut up. The sister thrush in the willow grove could be either Tsangyang Gyatso's lover, or a female helper or a go-between.

65

Serpent-demons bring various unpleasant illnesses. Plucking fruit in Indo-Tibetan love poetry, as perhaps in English, also connotes sexual intercourse (what is sometimes called 'making love', although all too often nowadays love doesn't seem to enter into it). Here, wonderfully for a Buddhist writer, Tsangyang Gyatso indicates that he is willing to go for the short-term pleasure regardless of the dangers in the longer term. Compare with verse 47. But maybe the serpent-demon is coming.

66

One rather doubts that this verse is by Tsangyang Gyatso! It is a nice Buddhist moralistic verse to put at the end of the collection. It recalls an old Buddhist story. The Buddha's disciple Ānanda is said to have asked the Buddha what a monk should do if a woman comes along. 'Don't look', was the reply. But what if it is already too late? 'Don't speak'. But what if they should speak? 'Then watch your mind carefully, Ānanda!'[21] But for poor Tsangyang Gyatso it was already far too late.

The Mind of a Dalai Lama

What I want to do here is something very speculative. For some it might even be considered a sort of blasphemy. I want to speculate more precisely on what the Sixth Dalai Lama's psychological problem was. There are those who consider that as the Dalai Lama he could not have had a psychological problem, and the appearance of inner problems is merely because, as a manifestation of Avalokiteśvara, he is beyond our ordinary understanding. In this vein we might cite a Tibetan verse:

> Who can rightly fathom the full extent
> of the appearance in all directions
> Of the illusory body of Padmapāṇi [Avalokiteśvara] in
> manifestations fitting
> To the diverse sight, pure and impure,
> of beings
> In the Land of Snow, the field of emanation
> of the Exalted One [Avalokiteśvara][1]

But however we look at it, even for the most pious Buddhist the Sixth Dalai Lama was a human being as well, with a human physiology and influenced by and influencing his historical circumstances. One can take it that physiologically his brain worked the same way as that of the rest of us. He should thus be open to the normal tools of the scholar, and the justification for scholarly investigation lies in the extent to which it enables us to understand the phenomena available to it. It seems clear (and the Thirteenth and Fourteenth Dalai Lamas confirm this) that the Sixth Dalai Lama was politically a disaster. Also he does not appear from his verses to have been a very happy man. That, it seems to me, means that (like all of us) he had problems. And some of those problems appear to have been inner. They were in part, I think, psychological or psycho-pharmacological.

I have suggested that the behaviour of Tsangyang Gyatso was in many ways that of a typical adolescent. But I think there is more that might explain the particular form his behaviour took under the circumstances. But what I have to say *is* highly speculative. That is why I have put it into an Appendix.

We do have some indication from the verses themselves what the Sixth Dalai Lama's problems might have been. I want to refer to verse 31:

nor bu rang la yod dus
nor bu'i nor nyams ma chod
nor bu mi la shor dus
snying rlung stod la tshangs byung

When I had the jewel,
I prized it not a jot.
When lost to another,
Depression broke my health.

The Tibetan *snying rlung stod la tshangs byung* in the last line is a technical expression of Tibetan medicine. It refers to illness brought on by a particular malfunction of the 'heart-wind'. Wind (*rlung*) disorders in Tibetan medicine cover a range of illnesses including psychiatric and psychosomatic problems.[2] When this and verses 32–3 are taken together, I would hazard a guess that the Dalai Lama was troubled by what is known in Tibetan medicine as a disorder of the 'pervasive wind'. This wind is located mainly in the heart according to the traditions of Tibetan medicine based on the Old Translations (rNying ma; pronounced 'Nying ma'). Others, such as the dGe lugs, would be inclined to locate it mainly in the head.[3] But given the family background of the Sixth Dalai Lama it is not surprising to find him on medicine following the Old Translations, the 'Ancient Ones'. Ostensibly the Dalai Lama has lost a particular lovely young woman to another person. He now blames himself. He did not value such a jewel enough. It looks as if guilt, anger and so on have brought on depression, in turn leading to other psychosomatic ailments and making him thoroughly ill. In Tibetan medicine disorder of the pervasive wind can be brought on by (among other things):

> shock, fright, depression, or phobic behavior. Symptoms include general wasting, insomnia, and decreased mental functioning as evidenced by prolonged staring and gaping, fainting, excessive verbal activity, and unsubstantiated fears.[4]

Judging by the verses, this looks close to the experience of the Dalai Lama. But recent scientific research into phenomena like anxiety, depression, phobias and compulsive addictions (including addictions to alcohol, gambling and sex) have linked them closely and convincingly with depletion of the brain chemical serotonin. This is a chemical the presence of which is associated with, and responsible for, feelings of ease and relaxation. Serotonin depletion commonly occurs as a result of long-term anxiety-inducing pressures. The early experiences of Tsangyang Gyatso are now recognized as precisely the sort of phenomena that might induce severe serotonin depletion in even the strongest of individuals. These include long-term house arrest, deprivation of his family, enormous pressure, constant expectations of cleverness, saintliness and learning, fears of assassination, death of his father, a tough mother, a demanding relationship with the fearsome Regent. They include all the other hundred and one things that we have seen in the life of the Sixth Dalai Lama. Interestingly fasting, starvation and an insufficient diet also lower serotonin levels. Moreover extensive research has shown that a situation where one is constantly being compared unfavourably with others, or compares oneself unfavourably to others, is a particular factor in lowering serotonin levels in certain people.[5] This is exactly the situation of Tsangyang Gyatso. Not only was he verbally and physically abused by the two local governors, but was subjected constantly to expectations that he would be as clever and as dominant as the Fifth Dalai Lama – the great hero of the Regent, who was himself a terribly clever man. At least some of those acquainted with him – but most of all the formidable Regent – were looking to see the return of the Great Fifth Dalai Lama. All were looking to see something special in a young lad identified as a reincarnation of a distinguished previous teacher.

So what I am suggesting is that we can be more precise than simply saying that the sort of upbringing Tsangyang Gyatso had explains his subsequent behaviour. I am suggesting that as a result of serotonin depletion the Sixth Dalai Lama suffered from symptoms of depression and quite possibly severe anxiety. This perhaps manifested itself in particular forms of compulsive or neurotic behaviour. He probably had little patience, and was possibly anxious about routine and ceremony. He may well have had panic attacks in crowds or in circumstances where he felt hemmed-in. He was also quite possibly actually addicted to sex, alcohol and gambling (at archery). He might have had a high level of aggression, although it might not have manifested directly as aggression. These are all related to serotonin depletion.

Let me summarize here the structure of my argument in this speculative section. I want to argue the following:

1. We know from some of the Sixth Dalai Lama's verses that he suffered medical disturbances which he, using the terminology of Tibetan medicine, associated with malfunction of the 'heart-wind'.

2. I have suggested that this corresponds in Tibetan medicine to a disorder of the 'pervasive wind'.

3. Disorder of the pervasive wind is brought on by (inter alia) depression and fright. It manifests itself in depressive behaviour.

4. Extensive modern scientific research has shown a correlation between depression and low levels of the brain chemical serotonin.

5. Among the factors that can lead in some individuals to a lowering of serotonin are a poor diet and long-term anxiety-inducing pressure, particularly in early life. A particularly potent form of this anxiety-inducing pressure is negative comparison. These (and others) are exactly the pressures the Sixth Dalai Lama experienced in early life.

6. I am thus suggesting that it is plausible that Tsangyang Gyatso had particularly low levels of serotonin. This would have led to forms of depression, possibly associated with addictions to alcohol, sex and gambling. Thus rather than depression being brought on by losing his girlfriend, the Dalai Lama's interest in girls may have been a symptom of his depression.

7. I am also suggesting that if he did suffer from low levels of serotonin, he might have experienced other phenomena that commonly go with it, such as acute anxiety, panic attacks, aggression, feelings of inadequacy, inability to cope, and so on.

Of course, we can never know. But that does not mean that we cannot speculate, and the speculation may help us to understand more fully this most tragic of Dalai Lamas as a human being like the rest of us. In seeing Tsangyang Gyatso as suffering from the psychophysical results of serotonin depletion we can not only understand and sympathize with him better. By looking at the various forms in which serotonin depletion manifests itself, such as social phobia or panic attacks, it may enable us to suggest, in the absence of further evidence, hypotheses and hypothetical behaviour that would explain events in the life of the Sixth Dalai Lama. And I suggest that this is very much a job for the historian.

ཆ ཆ ཆ ཆ ཆ

Notes

Introduction

[1] Sir Charles Bell, *Portrait of the Dalai Lama* (London: Collins, 1946), p 37.

[2] For more on this see Paul Williams and Anthony Tribe, *Buddhist Thought: A Complete Introduction to the Indian Tradition* (London and New York: Routledge, 2000), pp 4–6. For those unfamiliar with the field, this book could serve as an introduction to the whole Indian Buddhist background to the Sixth Dalai Lama's verses.

[3] Translated from the Tibetan. For an alternative translation of the whole of Atiśa's work, with a commentary attributed to him, see Atīśa, *A Lamp for the Path and Commentary*, trans. Richard Sherburne S.J. (London: George Allen and Unwin, 1983). This material can be found on p 5.

[4] Translated from the Sanskrit version by Kate Crosby and Andrew Skilton, in *Śāntideva: The Bodhicaryāvatāra* (Oxford and New York: Oxford University Press, 1995), 1:26. 'Mind' here means the Awakening Mind.

[5] *Ibid.*, 10:55.

[6] For details see Paul Williams, *Mahāyāna Buddhism: The Doctrinal Foundations* (London and New York: Routledge, 1989), pp 197–204.

[7] John F. Avedon, *Interview with the Dalai Lama* (New York: Littlebird, 1980), p 23. On not speaking about inner realizations, see p 21.

[8] See Dalai Lama, His Holiness the Fourteenth, *Āryaśūra's Aspiration and a Meditation on Compassion*, trans. Brian Beresford et al (Dharamsala: Library of Tibetan Works and Archives, 1979), p III. For an extensive discussion of the bodhisattva in Mahāyāna Buddhism see Williams, *Mahāyāna Buddhism*, ch. 9.

[9] See the interview with Tendzin Chögyal in Daniel Bärlocher, *Testimonies of Tibetan Tulkus: A Research among Reincarnate Buddhist Masters in Exile* (Rikon: Tibet-Institut, Opuscula Tibetana, 1982), vol I, p 215. This two-volume work of interviews with contemporary trulkus, almost exclusively of the Dalai Lama's dGe lugs school, is still by far the most important source on the subject.

[10] Claude B. Levenson, *The Dalai Lama: A Biography*, trans. Stephen Cox (London, Sydney, Wellington: Unwin Hyman, 1988), p 130.

[11] Tibetan, like many Asian languages, uses honorific words when referring to people or things considered in some way superior to the speaker.

[12] For a discussion of the 'Bodies of the Buddhas' see Williams, *Mahāyāna Buddhism*, ch. 8. For a shorter treatment see Williams and Tribe, *Buddhist Thought*, ch. 6.

[13] From the Chinese version of the *Gaṇḍavyūha Sūtra*, trans. Thomas Cleary in *The Flower Ornament Scripture*, vol 3 (Boston: Shambhala, 1987), p 152.

[14] Bärlocher, *Testimonies of Tibetan Tulkus*, vol I, pp 683–5.

[15] *Bod rgya tshig mdzod chen mo* (Beijing: Nationalities Publishing House, 1985), vol 2: *bla ma che gras kyi yang srid la btags pa'i ming*.

[16] See, for example, the definition of *sprul pa* in the Great Dictionary, which makes it clear that the term refers to what is normally thought of as the *nirmāṇakāyas* (i.e. *sprul sku*-s) of the Buddhas: *nang chos nas 'byung ba'i sangs rgyas kyi sku'i rnam 'phrul te / mchog gi sprul sku / skye ba sprul sku / bzo sprul sku / sna tshogs sprul sku lta bu /*. For more on some of these types of Buddha emanations see Williams, *Mahāyāna Buddhism*, pp 178–9, 182.

[17] Avedon, *Interview with the Dalai Lama*, p 23.

[18] This phenomenon, of looking for the reincarnation of a teacher, finding the child, and bringing the child back to his or her spiritual home, is found only in Tibetan Buddhism (including the Buddhism influenced by Tibet, like that of Mongolia). Why it developed here, alone in the Buddhist world, is an interesting question, but not for now.

[19] Dalai Lama, His Holiness the Fourteenth, *Freedom in Exile: The Autobiography of the Dalai Lama of Tibet* (London, Sydney, Auckland, Toronto: Hodder and Stoughton, 1990), p 236.

[20] Bärlocher, *Testimonies of Tibetan Tulkus*, vol 1, pp 286–7.

[21] Avedon, *Interview with the Dalai Lama*, p 59.

[22] Bärlocher, *Testimonies of Tibetan Tulkus*, vol 1, pp 682–3.

[23] Note the interesting discussion (Bärlocher, *Testimonies of Tibetan Tulkus*, vol 1, pp 255 ff) with Dakpo Tulku, another trulku who has given up the monastic life and now lives in Paris. Dakpo Tulku says quite categorically that he doubts he is of the same consciousness-stream as the great teacher of which he is supposed to be the reincarnation. He doubts this even though he was supposedly correctly identified and confirmed by the Dalai Lama. He is rather unhappy with the suggestion that he is therefore doubting the judgement of the Dalai Lama. He feels that the latter could not have made a mistake, but perhaps he had a perfectly justifiable reason for selecting him as Dakpo Tulku even though he is not literally the reincarnation of the previous Dakpo Tulku.

[24] Bärlocher, *Testimonies of Tibetan Tulkus*, vol 1, p 646.

[25] See, for example, the attempt by the Mongolian lama Dharmatāla to explain away another possible case in the early eighteenth century, relating to the Sixth and Seventh Dalai Lamas themselves, in Piotr Klafkowski trans., *The Secret Deliverance of the Sixth Dalai Lama, as Narrated by Dharmatāla* (Vienna: Arbeitskreis für Tibetische und Buddhistische Studien Universität Wien, Wiener Studien zur Tibetologie und Buddhismuskunde Heft 3, 1979), p 46. Avalokiteśvara can manifest in numerous forms at the same time.

[26] Bärlocher, *Testimonies of Tibetan Tulkus*, vol 1, p 351.

[27] *Ibid.*, p 251.

[28] Of course, I am ignoring throughout the philosophical issues that arise out of the whole idea of reincarnation and the verification of purported cases of reincarnation. There is a major issue of what it would be to verify a reincarnation claim, and whether meditative experience could do such a thing. I am also not going to discuss here the interesting and complex issue of what 'reincarnation' means in Buddhism, a religion that denies the existence of an unchanging, really existent referent for the concept 'I', what is usually called the 'Self' (and perhaps by some, the 'Soul'). For a philosophically and Buddhologically aware discussion of some of these issues see Steven Collins, *Selfless Persons: Imagery and Thought in Theravāda Buddhism* (Cambridge, London, New York, New Rochelle, Melbourne, Sydney: Cambridge University Press, 1982). Another topic is the various 'tests' that are used in Tibetan Buddhism to discover a genuine reincarnation. For a discussion of this see the present Dalai Lama's autobiographies.

[29] Williams, *Mahāyāna Buddhism*, pp 192–3.

[30] Bärlocher, *Testimonies of Tibetan Tulkus*, p 252.

[31] Dalai Lama, His Holiness the Fourteenth, *Tibet, China and the World: A Compilation of Interviews* (Dharamsala: Narthang Publications, 1989), p 1.

[32] One might think that the Fifth Dalai Lama in fact declared his 'Avalokiteśvara status' purely for political reasons, as a form of the divine right of kings. This would, I think, be too cynical. A book by Samten Karmay (*Secret Visions of the Fifth Dalai Lama* (London: Serindia Publications, 1988)), based on a recently discovered work by the Fifth Dalai Lama, shows that he was throughout his life subject to the most extraordinary series of visions. In 1663, we are told, the Fifth Dalai Lama received 'prophetic instructions on how to maintain the stability of the theocratic government'. In the evening of the same day, he felt his body transforming into that of a mansion containing Avalokiteśvara (pp 57–8). It would be quite wrong to suppose that the political advantages of discovering that he was closely connected with Avalokiteśvara meant that the Dalai Lama

did not really believe it and made up the 'revelation'. Quite the reverse.

[33] Dalai Lama, *Tibet, China and the World*, p 31.

[34] Levenson, *The Dalai Lama*, p 24; Michael Harris Goodman, *The Last Dalai Lama: A Biography* (London: Sidgwick and Jackson, 1986), p 337.

[35] Thus in fact splitting the consciousness continuum in a way often speculated about purely hypothetically in contemporary Western philosophy of mind.

[36] Goodman, *The Last Dalai Lama*, p 337.

[37] Bärlocher, *Testimonies of Tibetan Tulkus*, vol 1, p 663.

[38] Dalai Lama, *Freedom in Exile*, p 12.

[39] Bärlocher, *Testimonies of Tibetan Tulkus*, vol 1, pp 686–7.

[40] Avedon, *Interview with the Dalai Lama*, pp 58–9.

[41] Levenson, *The Dalai Lama*, p 182.

[42] Bärlocher, *Testimonies of Tibetan Tulkus*, vol 1, p 452.

[43] Avedon, *Interview with the Dalai Lama*, p 23.

[44] Dalai Lama, *Tibet, China and the World*, p 1, my italics.

[45] For the meditation practice see Dalai Lama, *Āryaśūra's Aspiration*, pp 92–3. The first autobiography reference is to Dalai Lama, *My Land and My People* (New York: Potala Corporation, 1977), p 195.

[46] The Dalai Lama speaks of Avalokiteśvara as his 'Master' perhaps as his brother Tendzin Chögyal speaks rather jokingly of the Buddha as 'the boss' by whom he as a trulku has been sent (Bärlocher, *Testimonies of Tibetan Tulkus*, vol 1, p 211).

[47] Goodman, *The Last Dalai Lama*, pp 325, 337.

[48] See Michael Aris, *Hidden Treasures and Secret Lives: A Study of Pemalingpa (1450–1521) and the Sixth Dalai Lama (1683–1706)* (Delhi, Varanasi, Patna, Bangalore, Madras: Motilal Banarsidass, Indian Institute of Advanced Study (Shimla), 1988), p 164. See also Helmut Hoffmann, *The Religions of Tibet*, trans. Edward Fitzgerald (London: George Allen and Unwin, 1961), p 180, where he speaks of the 'spirit of Avalokiteśvara' leaving the body of the Dalai Lama. This is a rather interpretive and faintly un-Buddhist notion. Perhaps Hoffmann was influenced here by Sir Charles Bell's translation of

byang chub in the same context as the 'spirit of enlightenment'; see Sir Charles Bell, *The Religion of Tibet* (Oxford: Clarendon Press, 1931; reprinted Oxford University Press, 1968, 1970), p 140. But technically that is a poor translation.

[49] Bell, *The Religion of Tibet*, p 126.

[50] It was common in Tibetan diplomacy to add in an oral message something that enhanced or supplemented any written text. In not writing it down it would not run the risk of falling into enemy hands, or in some other way compromising its source. We cannot be sure that this oral supplement did not in fact originate with the Fifth Dalai Lama himself.

[51] Thus when the Manchu Chinese emperor invited the Fifth Dalai Lama to visit him in China, it seems that the emperor himself – quite contrary to proper Chinese protocol – advanced to meet him. They related effectively on equal terms of mutual respect. At least, that is how the Tibetans (unlike the Chinese) have always seen and portrayed it.

[52] Tsepon W.D. Shakabpa, *Tibet: A Political History* (New York: Potala Publications, 1984), p 123.

[53] Quoted in Bell, *Portrait of the Dalai Lama*, p 34.

[54] Shakabpa, *Tibet: A Political History*, p 123.

[55] *Ibid.*, p 125. See also T.J. Norbu and Colin Turnbull, *Tibet: Its History, Religion and People* (Harmondsworth: Penguin Books, 1972), p 286.

[56] Aris, *Hidden Treasures and Secret Lives*, p 123.

[57] Quoted in *ibid.*, p 123.

[58] In the course of his researches on Bhutanese history, Michael Aris discovered that the death of the *Zhabs drung* of Bhutan (d. *c.*1651) was kept secret in a similar way and at about the same time for over 50 years. Perhaps the Tibetan Regent knew of this precedent. See Aris, *Bhutan: The Early History of a Himalayan Kingdom* (Warminster: Aris and Philips, 1979), pt 3.

[59] In fact, one of the great problems with the Tibetan system of 'rule by reincarnation' is the power it gives to any regent during the inevitably long period of a ruler's minority.

[60] Quoted in Aris, *Hidden Treasures and Secret Lives*, p 129.

[61] *Ibid.*, p 134.

[62] *Ibid.*, p 139.

[63] On its translation, see my comments on verse 54.

[64] Aris, *Hidden Treasures and Secret Lives*, p 147.

[65] *Ibid.*, p 154.

[66] Shakabpa, *Tibet: A Political History*, p 130.

[67] Quoted in Aris, *Hidden Treasures and Secret Lives*, p 159.

[68] Bell, *Portrait of the Dalai Lama*, p 66.

[69] Norbu and Turnbull, *Tibet: Its History, Religion and People*; Helmut Hoffmann, 'Historical introduction' to G.W. Houston (trans.), *Wings of the White Crane: Poems of Tshangs dbyangs rgya mtsho (1683–1706)* (Delhi, Varanasi, Patna: Motilal Banarsidass, 1982).

[70] *gong re nang mo med pa nyal ma myong / thig le gnyung dkar tsam zhig gtong ma myong.*

[71] Norbu and Turnbull, *Tibet: Its History, Religion and People*, pp 291–2.

[72] On the dGe lugs interpretation of the highest levels of tantric practice (i.e. the so-called *anuttarayogatantra*) see Daniel Cozort, *Highest Yoga Tantra* (Ithaca, NY: Snow Lion, 1986). On the use of a consort see especially p 88.

[73] Translated in K. Dhondup, *Songs of the Sixth Dalai Lama* (Dharamsala: Library of Tibetan Works and Archives, 1981), p 32.

[74] *Ibid.*, pp 38–9, 83.

[75] Melvyn C. Goldstein, *A History of Modern Tibet 1913–1951: The Demise of the Lamaist State* (Berkeley, Los Angeles, London: University of California Press, 1989), p 330.

[76] Quoted in Bell, *Portrait of the Dalai Lama*, p 37.

[77] Bell, *The Religion of Tibet*, p 141.

[78] Dalai Lama, *Tibet, China and the World*, p 31.

[79] Shakabpa, *Tibet: A Political History*, p 129.

[80] Hoffmann, 'Historical introduction', pp xvi ff, makes a great deal of a report sent back to the Chinese emperor by a Manchu general, Funingga, that attributes all kind of 'heretical' religious practices

(including sexual practices) to Tsangyang Gyatso. I agree with Aris (*Hidden Treasures and Secret Lives*, p 160) in being extremely sceptical of the veracity of this report. It is likely to have been a justification for the Dalai Lama's removal. Either way, it is difficult to see how a Manchu general writing to a Chinese emperor can give us much information on the Dalai Lama's supposedly 'secret' activities, and it is unlikely that we would find material in a report of this sort that is lacking in all other sources including those of the Tibetans themselves. Aris comments that 'Tsangyang Gyamtso's [sic] love for the ladies was all too human. He appears to have been a bold and honest rebel who would surely have laughed at such attempts to explain his behaviour, whether aimed at discrediting him or doing him honour.' I doubt that he can seriously be portrayed as 'a rebel', but I also doubt that Tsangyang Gyatso was anything other than an ordinary adolescent lover of young women.

[81] See Bell, *The Religion of Tibet*, pp 141–2, quoting a Tibetan friend.

[82] This verse, incidentally, also suggests that the strange verse quoted above concerning 'never loosing a single drop of sperm' could not be by the same author. Any explanation of the conduct of the Sixth Dalai Lama that would have recourse to advanced tantric practice that entails reversing the flow of orgasm, and thence semen, must contradict any explanation in terms of engendering a child.

[83] Compare with Communist China, and hence modern Tibet, which seems to have all the old puritanism of Marx's Europe.

[84] Per Sorensen, *Divinity Secularized: An Inquiry into the Nature and Form of the Songs Ascribed to the Sixth Dalai Lama* (Vienna: Arbeitskreis für Tibetische und Buddhistische Studien Universität Wien, Wiener Studien zur Tibetologie und Buddhismuskunde Heft 25, 1990), p 216.

[85] *Ibid.*, p 32.

[86] Melvyn C. Goldstein, 'Lhasa street songs: Political and social satire in traditional Tibet', *The Tibet Journal*, 7/1+2 (Spring/Summer, 1982).

[87] Aris, *Hidden Treasures and Secret Lives*, p 242.

[88] A point sometimes missed in the translations by Houston (and at least one case in Barks, presumably following Houston). This has laughable results, when lines five and six of one verse have sometimes been tagged on to lines one and two of the following verse, with knock-on consequences for some of the subsequent verses. The upshot is complete incoherence.

[89] For more on Tibetan metres see Stephan V. Beyer, *The Classical Tibetan Language* (Albany, NY: State University of New York Press, 1992), pp 408–23; Thupten Jinpa and Jaś Elsner, *Songs of Spiritual Experience: Tibetan Buddhist Poems of Insight and Awakening* (Boston and London: Shambhala, 2000), pp 13–14.

[90] Bell, *The Religion of Tibet*, p 138.

[91] Mark Tatz, 'Songs of the Sixth Dalai Lama', *The Tibet Journal*, 6/4 (Winter 1981).

[92] K. Dhondup, *Songs of the Sixth Dalai Lama*; italics original.

[93] G.W. Houston (trans.), *Wings of the White Crane: Poems of Tshangs dbyangs rgya mtsho (1683–1706)* (Delhi, Varanasi, Patna: Motilal Banarsidass, 1982).

[94] Per Sorensen, *Divinity Secularized*.

[95] Coleman Barks, *Stallion on a Frozen Lake: Love Songs of the Sixth Dalai Lama*, trans. Coleman Barks (Athens, GA: Maypop Books, 1992).

[96] Rick Fields and Brian Cutillo (trans.), *The Turquoise Bee: The Lovesongs of the Sixth Dalai Lama* (New York and San Francisco: HarperCollins, 1998).

Notes for Appreciation

[1] Per Sorensen, *Divinity Secularized*, p 47. All references to Sorensen are to this 1990 book and his commentary on the relevant verse.

[2] See Williams, *Mahāyāna Buddhism*, p 237; Williams and Tribe, *Buddhist Thought*, p 189.

[3] For more on Prajñāpāramitā and Madhyamaka, see Williams, *Mahāyāna Buddhism*, chs. 2–3; Williams and Tribe, *Buddhist Thought*, pp 131–52.

[4] See, for example, the *Pañcakrama* in Alex Wayman, *The Yoga of the Guhysamājatantra: The Arcane Lore of Forty Verses* (Delhi: Motilal Banarsidass, 1980), p 227.

[5] Aris, *Hidden Treasures and Secret Lives*, p 156.

[6] Bell, *The Religion of Tibet*, p 128.

[7] For a picture of such a boat see David Snellgrove and Hugh Richardson, *A Cultural History of Tibet* (London: Weidenfeld and Nicolson, 1968), p 168. Sorensen claims that the actual boat can be seen in the photograph in Bell, *The Religion of Tibet*, opposite p 138. This claim is based on it being the horse-headed boat in the lake by the *nāga* palace that the Sixth Dalai Lama had built in the gardens near the Potala. I do not know how it is possible to claim that this is the actual boat itself, after all these years. But I suppose it may be so.

[8] Tatz, 'Songs of the Sixth Dalai Lama'.

[9] Dhondup, *Songs of the Sixth Dalai Lama*, p 83.

[10] Sorensen, *Divinity Secularized*, p 139.

[11] *Ibid.*, p 126.

[12] *Ibid.*, p 132.

[13] See, for example, Robert B. Ekvall, *Religious Observances in Tibet: Patterns and Function* (Chicago and London: University of Chicago Press, 1964), ch. 9.

[14] See Aris, *Hidden Treasures and Secret Lives*, p 157.

[15] For more on Buddhist and Tibetan cosmology see Rupert Gethin, *The Foundations of Buddhism* (Oxford and New York: Oxford University Press, 1998), ch. 5, and Martin Brauen, *The Mandala: Sacred Circle in Tibetan Buddhism*, trans. Martin Wilson (Boston: Shambhala, 1998).

[16] See Barbara Stoler Miller (trans.), *Bhartrihari: Poems* (New York and London: Columbia University Press, 1967).

[17] Aris, *Hidden Treasures and Secret Lives*, p 153.

[18] For more on this see Williams and Tribe, *Buddhist Thought*, ch. 1.

[19] Aris, *Hidden Treasures and Secret Lives*, p 156.

[20] Ekvall, *Religious Observances in Tibet*, ch. 9.

[21] See the *Mahāparinibbāna Sutta*, ch. 5, sect. 9.

Appendix: The Mind of a Dalai Lama

[1] Translated in Aris, *Hidden Treasures and Secret Lives*, p 212.

[2] For an indication of the sort of phenomena included under wind disorders see Mark Epstein and Lobsang Rapgay, 'Mind and mental disorders in Tibetan Medicine', *gSo-Rig: Tibetan Medicine*, series no. 5 (1982).

[3] See Yeshi Donden, *Health Through Balance: An Introduction to Tibetan Medicine* (Ithaca, NY: Snow Lion, 1986), p 46.

[4] Epstein and Rapgay, 'Mind and mental disorders in Tibetan Medicine', p 78.

[5] I rely for my account of serotonin depletion and its effects on Oliver James, *Britain on the Couch: Treating a Low Serotonin Society* (London: Arrow Books, 1998). This work makes constant reference to the results of recent research. On the importance of negative comparison in inducing serotonin depletion, see in particular chapter 2. Because comparison is a relative matter, the effect of negative comparison is that even people who are relatively well off and privileged can suffer from low serotonin and the experiences that go with it. In the case of Tsangyang Gyatso, his discovery as the reincarnation of the Fifth Dalai Lama (even when it was known to only a few) would have increased almost immeasurably the pressures of negative comparison. On the association of low serotonin with addictive behaviour, including addition to alcohol, gambling and sex, see James's appendix 2.

ळ ळ ळ ळ ळ

Bibliography

Aris, Michael, *Bhutan: The Early History of a Himalayan Kingdom*
(Warminster: Aris and Phillips, 1979)
——, *Hidden Treasures and Secret Lives: A Study of Pemalingpa (1450–
1521) and the Sixth Dalai Lama (1683–1706)* (Delhi, Varanasi,
Patna, Bangalore, Madras: Motilal Banarsidass, Indian Institute
of Advanced Study (Shimla), 1988)
Atīśa, *A Lamp for the Path and Commentary*, trans. Richard Sher-
burne S.J. (London: George Allen and Unwin, 1983)
Avedon, John F., *Interview with the Dalai Lama* (New York:
Littlebird, 1980)
Barks, Coleman, *Stallion on a Frozen Lake: Love Songs of the Sixth
Dalai Lama*, trans. Coleman Barks (Athens, GA: Maypop
Books, 1992)
Bärlocher, Daniel, *Testimonies of Tibetan Tulkus: A Research among
Reincarnate Buddhist Masters in Exile*, 2 volumes (Rikon: Ti-
bet-Institut, Opuscula Tibetana, 1982)
Bell, Sir Charles, *The Religion of Tibet* (Oxford: Clarendon Press,
1931; reprinted Oxford University Press, 1968, 1970)
——, *Portrait of the Dalai Lama* (London: Collins, 1946)
Beyer, Stephan V., *The Classical Tibetan Language* (Albany, NY:
State University of New York Press, 1992)
Bod rgya tshig mdzod chen mo, Zhang Yi-sun (chief editor) (Beijing:
Nationalities Publishing House, 1985). Three volumes. English
of volume 1: *An Encyclopaedic Tibetan–English Dictionary (Ka-
Nya)*, trans. Gyurme Dorje and Tudeng Nima (Bei-
jing/London: Nationalities Publishing House/School of

Oriental and African Studies, 2001). Further volumes in preparation.

Brauen, Martin, *The Mandala: Sacred Circle in Tibetan Buddhism*, trans. Martin Wilson (Boston: Shambhala, 1998)

Collins, Steven, *Selfless Persons: Imagery and Thought in Theravāda Buddhism* (Cambridge, London, New York, New Rochelle, Melbourne, Sydney: Cambridge University Press, 1982)

Cozort, Daniel, *Highest Yoga Tantra* (Ithaca, NY: Snow Lion, 1986)

Crosby, Kate, and Andrew Skilton (trans.), *Śāntideva: The Bodhicaryāvatāra* (Oxford, New York: Oxford University Press, 1995)

Dalai Lama, His Holiness the Fourteenth, *My Land and My People* (New York: Potala Corp., 1977; first published by McGraw-Hill, 1962)

——, *Āryaśūra's Aspiration and a Meditation on Compassion*, trans. Brian Beresford et al (Dharamsala: Library of Tibetan Works and Archives, 1979)

——, *Tibet, China and the World: A Compilation of Interviews* (Dharamsala: Narthang Publications, 1989)

——, *Freedom in Exile: The Autobiography of the Dalai Lama of Tibet* (London, Sydney, Auckland, Toronto: Hodder and Stoughton, 1990)

Dhondup, K., *Songs of the Sixth Dalai Lama* (Dharamsala: Library of Tibetan Works and Archives, 1981)

Donden, Yeshi, *Health Through Balance: An Introduction to Tibetan Medicine* (Ithaca, NY: Snow Lion, 1986)

Ekvall, Robert B., *Religious Observances in Tibet: Patterns and Function* (Chicago and London: University of Chicago Press, 1964)

Epstein, Mark, and Lobsang Rapgay, 'Mind and mental disorders in Tibetan medicine', *gSo-Rig: Tibetan Medicine*, series no. 5 (1982)

Fields, Rick, and Brian Cutillo (trans.), *The Turquoise Bee: The Lovesongs of the Sixth Dalai Lama* (New York and San Francisco: HarperCollins, 1998)

Gaṇḍavyūha Sūtra, Chinese version translated in Thomas Cleary, *The Flower Ornament Scripture*, vol 3 (Boston: Shambhala, 1987)

Gethin, Rupert, *The Foundations of Buddhism* (Oxford and New York: Oxford University Press, 1998)

Goldstein, Melvyn C., 'Lhasa street songs: Political and social satire in traditional Tibet', *The Tibet Journal*, 7/1+2 (Spring/Summer, 1982)

——, *A History of Modern Tibet 1913–1951: The Demise of the Lamaist State* (Berkeley, Los Angeles, London: University of California Press, 1989)

Goodman, Michael Harris, *The Last Dalai Lama: A Biography* (London: Sidgwick and Jackson, 1986)

Hoffmann, Helmut, *The Religions of Tibet*, trans. Edward Fitzgerald (London: George Allen and Unwin, 1961)

——, 'Historical introduction' to G.W. Houston (trans.), *Wings of the White Crane: Poems of Tshangs dbyangs rgya mtsho (1683–1706)*

Houston, G.W. (trans.), *Wings of the White Crane: Poems of Tshangs dbyangs rgya mtsho (1683–1706)* (Delhi, Varanasi, Patna: Motilal Banarsidass, 1982)

James, Oliver, *Britain on the Couch: Treating a Low Serotonin Society* (London: Arrow Books, 1998)

Jinpa, Thupten, and Jaś Elsner, *Songs of Spiritual Experience: Tibetan Buddhist Poems of Insight and Awakening* (Boston and London: Shambhala, 2000)

Karmay, Samten Gyaltsen, *Secret Visions of the Fifth Dalai Lama* (London: Serindia Publications, 1988)

Klafkowski, Piotr (trans.), *The Secret Deliverance of the Sixth Dalai Lama, as Narrated by Dharmatāla* (Vienna: Arbeitskreis für Tibetische und Buddhistische Studien Universität Wien, Wiener Studien zur Tibetologie und Buddhismuskunde Heft 3, 1979)

Levenson, Claude B. *The Dalai Lama: A Biography*, trans. Stephen Cox (London, Sydney, Wellington: Unwin Hyman, 1988)

Norbu, Thubten Jigme, and Colin Turnbull, *Tibet: Its History, Religion and People* (Harmondsworth: Penguin Books, 1972)

Shakabpa, Tsepon W.D., *Tibet: A Political History* (New York: Potala Publications, 1984; first edition by Yale University Press, 1967)

Snellgrove, David, and Hugh Richardson, *A Cultural History of Tibet* (London: Weidenfeld and Nicolson, 1968)

Sorensen, Per, *Divinity Secularized: An Inquiry into the Nature and Form of the Songs Ascribed to the Sixth Dalai Lama* (Vienna: Arbeitskreis für Tibetische und Buddhistische Studien Universität Wien, Wiener Studien zur Tibetologie und Buddhismuskunde Heft 25, 1990)

Stoler Miller, Barbara (trans.), *Bhartrihari: Poems* (New York and London: Columbia University Press, 1967)

Tatz, Mark, 'Songs of the Sixth Dalai Lama', *The Tibet Journal*, 6/4 (Winter 1981)

Wayman, Alex, *The Yoga of the Guhyasamājatantra: The Arcane Lore of Forty Verses* (Delhi: Motilal Banarsidass, 1980; first edition by Samuel Weiser, New York, 1977)

Williams, Paul, *Mahāyāna Buddhism: The Doctrinal Foundations* (London and New York: Routledge, 1989)

Williams, Paul, with Anthony Tribe, *Buddhist Thought: A Complete Introduction to the Indian Tradition* (London and New York: Routledge, 2000)

ཨ ཨ ཨ ཨ ཨ

Line Index: Tibetan

kong phrug gzhon pa'i blo sna: 25b
kong yul mthil gyi ne tso: 60b
klu bdud rdo rje'i zil pa: 20b
dkar gos nang nas chod song: 44b
dkar gsal zla ba shar byung: 1b
bkra shis zla ba dkar po'i: 42c
skad cha smras ni mi shes: 26d
skya khra hor pas mi thub: 62d
skya ser rlung gi pho nya: 8b
skyur ba de dang 'dra byung: 4d
skye 'gro mi rtag 'chi ba: 47a

kha rog bzhugs rogs mdzod dang:
    64b
kham sdong mthon po'i rtse nas:
    5c
kham bu'i shing la skyes sam: 35b
khams 'bras mtshar la bltas na: 5b
khu byug mon nas yong bas: 46a
khong nang sems pa'i gcong gis:
    32c
khyi rgan rgya bo zer ba: 52a
khyi de stag khyi gzig khyi: 48a
khra bo'i sbrul la ma brgyab: 11c
khrel dang ngo tsha med na: 26b
khrel dang gzhung gi the 'u: 14c
khrel gzhung med pa'i byams pas:
    10c
'khrungs sa 'khrungs yul mi gcig:
    60c

ga ler phebs shig byas pas: 56c

ga ler bzhugs shig gsung gis: 56d
gru shan sems pa med kyang: 10a
dgongs su dag pa khag theg: 61b
mgo la rgyab pa'i gtsug gyus: 26c
mgyogs po 'phrad yong gsungs
    byung: 56f
mgron po la ni bos byung: 21d
'gro zhor lam bu'i snying thub: 4a
'grogs 'dris e yong dris pas: 23b
rgod po'i sgro la gzan byung: 38b
rgya gar shar gyi rma bya: 60a
rgya mtsho'i gting nas nor bu: 3c
rgyab kyi klu bdud btsan po: 65a
sgom pa'i bla ma zhal ras: 18a
brgyab pa'i nag chung the 'us: 14a

nga dang byams pa phrad nas: 46c
nga dang byams pa'i sdebs sa: 50a
nga dang tshong 'dus bu mo'i: 11a
nga ni skyo rgyu mi 'dug: 7d
nga la phyi mig mi lta: 10d
nga la gzan po byas byung: 38d
nga la yod pa'i chung 'dris: 51c
nga la gshog rtsal gyar dang: 57b
ngang pa 'dam la chags nas: 9a
ngan song myong dgos mi 'dug:
    20f
rngon pa rang gis zin kyang: 30b

bco lnga'i nam dang mnyam pa'i:
    44c
lcang ma byi 'ur sems shor: 62a

175

lcang ma'i logs la btsugs yod: 12b
lcang gling a lce 'jol mo: 64c
lcang srung a jo zhal ngos: 12c

chang ma ye shes mkha' 'gro: 20d
chang la 'dzad pa mi 'dug: 34b
chu dang thig pas 'jig song: 13b
chung 'dris byams pa'i rlung
    bskyed: 12a
chung 'dris byams par bshad pas:
    29b
chung 'dris byams pa 'phrad byung:
    59c
chos rgyal las kyi me long: 58b
mchod pa'i rdzas la phebs na: 15b
'chal po dwangs bzang dbang po:
    54d
'chi bral byed na min na: 23c

mjal 'dzom e yong blta'o: 63d
'jigs dang mi 'jigs mi 'dug: 65b

nyi ma zla ba'i bskor phyogs: 43c
nyin mo lag tu ma lon: 6c
gnyis pa ma 'dris chog pa: 66c
rnyi dang zhags pas zin gyis: 37b
snying gtam pha mar ma bshad:
    29a
snying gtam bshad sa ma red: 40d
snying nas ma dran zer na: 47b
snying nas sha tsha yod med: 27c
snying rlung stod la tshangs byung:
    31d

gtan gyi mdun mar byung na: 3b
gtan grogs khyod la bsams pa'i: 26a
rta mgos phyi mig bltas byung: 10b
rta rgod ri la rgyab pa: 37a
rta pho gtong sa ma red: 40b
rting ma byis pa'i lo la: 63c
rting ma'i zla ba tshur yong: 42b
stong ldan ha lo'i me tog: 15a
bstan pa'i dgra bo sgrol dang: 45d

thag ring rgyang la mi 'gro: 57c
thugs sems skyo yong byas pas: 56e
tho rangs kha ba bab byung: 53d
tho rangs log byung ma zer: 52d
mthu ngo zin pa mi 'dug: 37d
mthu dang nus pa yod na: 45c
'thogs su dgos pa byas song: 65d

da lta'i tshe thung 'di la: 63a
da lo sog ma'i phon lcog: 2b
dag pa shel ri gangs chu: 20a
dang po ma mthong chog pa: 66a
dam can rdo rje chos skyong: 45b
dam tshig gtsang mas btung na:
    20e
dam pa'i chos la phebs na: 16b
dam pa'i chos la phyin na: 19b
de kha tsam zhig zhus nas: 63b
de nas khrig khrig gnang zhu: 58d
don la lkugs pa 'dra byung: 47d
bdud rtsi sman gyi phab rgyun: 20c
mda' mo 'ben la phog song: 59a
mdun gyi ka ra ku shu: 65c
mde'u sa la 'dzul song: 59b
'di na khrig khrig mi 'dug: 58c
'di la bcol bas los chog: 34d
'dris nas mthu ru langs song: 48d
rdo ka rgyag pa ma gnang: 12d
ldag kha ster nas 'dris song: 48b

na ning btab pa'i ljang gzhon: 2a
nang gi stag mo ral 'dzoms: 48c
nam mkha'i skar tshod thig byung:
    49d
nor bu mi la shor dus: 31c
nor bu rang la yod dus: 31a
nor bu'i nor nyams ma chod: 31b
nor bzang rgyal bus 'phrogs song:
    30d
nor yong bsam pa mi 'dug: 43d
gnam lo'i sa bcud 'phel song: 46b
gnas mo'i nang la thal song: 61d
rnam shes mi las spyang ba: 52b

Line Index: English

First, better not to see: 66a
Flowering's time has fled: 7a
Foes have learned my secrets: 29d
Folk gossip about me: 61a
Footprints left in the snow: 53d
For my love from childhood: 12a
For that passionate girl: 33c
Frozen ground, surface slips: 40a
Frustration's my sole friend: 6d

Girl with the fragrant limbs: 4b
'Goodbye', was her response: 56d
Gorgeous hollyhock blooms: 15a
Green shoots planted last year: 2a
Guardian of Willows: 12c

Has married another: 32b
He is going to die: 41d
Heading forth, a hermit: 24c
Heart-talk's not for parents: 29a
He'd bedded her three days: 25a
Held by the King of Hell: 58b
Here, it's just not been right: 58c
He's behind. But who cares: 65b
Hoarfrost sugars the grass: 8a
Holy Lhasa they meet: 60d
Hope too flew far away: 9d
Hoped to remain awhile: 9b

I and my love have met: 46c
I asked for holy help: 17b
I become a Buddha: 19d
I belie my girl's heart: 24d
I can surmise the stars: 49b
I can't measure her mood: 49d
I feel just devoured: 38c
I lose life's religion: 24b
I lose my sleep at night: 6b
I prized it not a jot: 31b
I sought my love at dusk: 53a
I, too, am not staying: 16c
I too shall not lament: 7d
I, too – young turquoise bee: 15c

I was invited home: 21c
If given in worship: 15b
If my sweetheart won't stay: 16a
If she who stole my heart: 3a
If the girl doesn't die: 34a
If there should be issue: 28c
If you say you don't heed: 47a
'I'll miss you', he told her: 56e
I'll not go far. Circling: 57c
I'm straight off on retreat: 16d
In mind, so clearly clear: 18d
In our next childhood's years: 63d
In Potala dwelling: 54a
In sun and moon's orbit: 43d
In the topmost branches: 5d
In this short present life: 63a
Indeed, I can name her: 34c
Is a southern forest: 50b
Is from its very midst: 51d
Is no place for heart-talk: 40d
It is known by no one: 50c
It seems like the full moon: 41b
It's for an old friend. But: 29b
Its head was in the ground: 59b

Lady, a Lord's daughter: 5a
Laughing smiles, with white teeth:
  22b
Leading on the youth's mind: 27b
Lend the strength of your wings:
  57b
Let's see whether we meet: 63c
Lhasa and Zhol roaming: 54c
Lhasa is crowded. Still: 51a
Like a bee in a web: 25b
Like finding rare turquoise: 4c
Like landing a jewel: 3c
Lithang, I shall return 57d
Long-maned indoor-tigress: 48c
Luderdorje dewdrops: 20b

Meditating – in mind: 18a
Meru, king of mountains: 43a

ॐ ॐ ॐ ॐ ॐ

Name and Subject Index

Note: Tibetan words are indexed under their pronounced rather than transliterated form.

Dorje (Tibetan *rDo rje*) 'thunder-
bolt', or 'diamond', a common
term in Tantric contexts,
sometimes also used for personal
names, 56
Dorje Drakden (Tibetan *rDo rje
grags ldan*), the Dalai Lama's
protector-deity, 56
Drepung (Tibetan *'Bras spungs*),
Gelukba (*dGe lugs pa*) monas-
tery, 25, 38
Dzungars, Mongol clan in rivalry
to the Khoshuud (Qoshot)
Mongols, 37–8, 39

Epstein, M., 170

Fields, R., 51, 57–8
Funingga, Manchu general, 166–7

Ganden (Tibetan *dGa' ldan*),
Geluk (*dGe lugs*) monastery, 23,
26
Geluk (Tibetan *dGe lugs*), school
of Tibetan Buddhism
foundation, 9
history, 25–6, 27, 28
leadership of, 23
medical traditions, 156
moral code, 42
philosophy of, 128
and virtue, 20–1
Gendun Cherpel (Tibetan *dGe
'dun chos phel*, d. 1951), twenti-
eth-century dGe lugs pa with a
reputation for 'freethinking' and
iconoclastic behaviour, 36
Gongbo (Tibetan *Kong po*, or
Kong yul), a district near Lhasa,
140
Gonsar Tulku, 13

'Great Tibetan–Chinese Diction-
ary' *see Bod rgya tshig mdzod chen
mo*
Grueber, Johannes, Austrian
Jesuit, 28
Guhyasamāja Tantra, a Tantric
scripture, 128
Gushri Khan, (d. 1655), Khoshuud
(Qoshot) Mongol leader and
supporter of the Fifth Dalai
Lama, 27, 29
Gyatso, Tsangyang, Sixth Dalai
Lama (Tibetan *Tshangs dbyangs
rgya mtsho*) *see* Dalai Lama,
Sixth

Hlorong (Tibetan *Lho rong*),
region in the south of Tibet, on
the borders with India, 149
Hoffmann, H., 41, 164–5, 166–7
Houston, G. W., 57, 168

India, 39, 153

James, Oliver, 170
Japanese poetry, 145
Jetsun Dampa of Urga (Tibetan
rJe btsun dam pa), the leading
dGe lugs teacher in Mongolia,
40–1, 44
Jigdal Sakya Rinpoche, 16
Jo nang pa, school of Tibetan
Buddhism apparently suppressed
by the Fifth Dalai Lama, 28

Kagyer (Tibetan *bKa' brgyud*),
school of Tibetan Buddhism
Karma sub-school, 25–6, 27, 28
Drukpa (Tibetan *'Brug pa*) sub-
school, 137
K'ang-hsi (1661–1722), Ch'ing
Chinese emperor, 34
Karmay, Samten, 163